Y0-BTD-992

Higher
Education
in the European
Community

Higher Education in the European Community

Reform and Economics

Eric Bockstael
Paris

Otto Feinstein
Monteith College
Wayne State University

Heath Lexington Books
D. C. Heath and Company
Lexington, Massachusetts

Printed in the United States of America

Library of Congress Number: 78-129155

Table of Contents

List of Tables

Preface

This study of the development of higher education in the European Economic Community is part of a larger comparative study of planning, quality, and personalism, directed by Otto Feinstein and funded by the Danforth Foundation. The studies compare the problems of United States and continental European higher education. The basic research and writing of this part of the study was done by Eric Bockstael. At the time of writing certain basic reforms of secondary and higher education were being considered, and in some cases being applied, in the European Economic Community. Radical questioning of the content of higher education and the structure of the university was confined to small left-wing groups in Germany, at the Free University of Berlin, and in France. Since then we have had an extraordinary eruption of student confrontation at continental universities, in some ways overshadowing similar dramatic events in the United States. The May-June explosion of 1968 began as a student movement and had among its consequences the resignation and political retirement of General Charles de Gaulle.

This study deals with the conditions in higher education which make the dramatic student movements of the most recent past in France, Germany, Italy, the Netherlands and Belgium comprehensible. The problem of democratization, of opening the university to children from the working class, can in some ways be compared to the problem of opening the university to nonwhite students in the United States, though in this comparison we see some essential differences in the two societies. The change in curriculum and structure of the university to deal with the growing importance of technology and applied social sciences in Europe might be compared to the American problem of making the multiversity sensitive to the needs of its students and its surrounding society. But again in this comparison we will see mirrored the difference in the two societies. The challenge to function and structure of the American and European university thus reflect different societies in the process of dramatic change. A new dimension is added to our study of the economics of higher education, of planning, and of the consequences to educational quality and personalism in the educational environment, as we investigate similar issues in such different environments.

The events which have occurred since the completion of our study only add weight to our findings. The May-June revolt in France led to a major reform in higher education, which, however, has met with great resistance manifested by repeated strikes in the various universities, even those created by the reform law. The crisis of the French, Italian, and to a lesser degree, the German university has now become a general crisis of the respective society. Economic growth, no longer exclusively dependent upon the accumulation of capital and the utilization of labor in the industrial sector, but more than ever dependent on technological development, research, new methods of management, the capacity to foresee, to plan and to organize, challenges the university with a new but most critical role in society. The new role of the university is inseparable from social and political transformation of the society. The organization of education and research are critical issues, raising basic questions of priorities and power, determining the direction in which society will go.

It is no longer sufficient to explain the crisis of the university in terms of the malfunctioning of the institution, of the selection process which resulted in only a small increase of graduates despite the unprecedented expansion of higher education, the inflexibility of curricula or teaching methods, or the high dropout rate. This new understanding on the part of students and intellectuals was already being formed in 1966. The various discussions we report in our last chapter reveal the profound anxiety and frustration which has led to the confrontations we witnessed two years later in France, Germany, and Italy. It also explains why a simple modernization of education, or its adaptation to the technocratic requirements of the economy did not and could not resolve the crisis. French writer and philosopher, Jean-Paul Sartre, in an interview we had with him following the May-June revolt, underlined what he considered the most fundamental change in the university movement:

In the early sixties the students were very political and they had, for the most part, clearly defined positions as citizens, not as students, particularly as regarded the war in Algeria. They simply thought that, as young people, as intellectuals, they had to intervene in the life of the society and take a stand on the great issues of the day. Today, it is quite different. They are questioning themselves. They consider themselves as marginal elements destined to enter a society which they do not want because they have understood its character and realize the role that they are designed to play in it. Consequently they revolt like workers do, that is for reasons which have to do with their own alienation and not to help the oppressed Algerian people.

It is a similar analysis which led André Malraux, then Minister of Culture, to remark, that the May-June explosion was only a general rehearsal for a world drama to come which could not be altered by the institutionalization of change or the differentiation of university structure designed to facilitate initiative and thus limit the revolts.

The question of the structure and function of the university has clearly become intertwined with the general crisis of European society and civilization. Our study, designed to deal with the former, thus offers a first historical perspective in the development of the crisis of higher education in Europe. We hope that this first study will be followed up, opening areas of further investigation, particularly with respect to the planning methods, the problem of democratization, and an analysis of the period of revolt and paralysis which has occurred since our original study. We wish to thank the Danforth Foundation for its generous grant, without which this study could not have been undertaken.

**Higher
Education
in the European
Community**

1 The Problematic

Europe is at the doorstep of a second industrial revolution characterized by increasing automation and a more extensive use of computers, bringing about a shift in the division of labor, with an ever increasing percentage of the active population occupied in the tertiary sector (services); a slight increase tending towards stabilization in the secondary sector, and a continuous decrease in the primary sector; stimulating an overall economic expansion and rising standards of living, increasing the consumption of material goods as well as services, heading towards an evolution which one has observed in the United States during the last few years where the family's expenditures are more and more oriented towards services.

Man is building, through his increased scientific knowledge and with the help of constantly developing techniques, a society in which there would be better living standards and in which a greater place would be given to culture, no longer reserved to a few but open to all, and where personal aptitudes would be the only limits.

These rapid transformations of the modern world necessitate a profound change in the methods of education. In former times, the school's role was to give the pupils a limited number of basic elements (reading, writing, calculating) to enable them to insert themselves satisfactorily into the production sector. At the secondary and higher levels of education – to which only children coming from the higher social classes were directed – one trained "honnêtes hommes" (in the sense in which it was understood by 17th century classicism) and professional training was considered less important.

Today, however, with the extraordinary university expansion due to social demand and the needs of a growing economy, we see various power groups – state (administration), business, industry, and students, etc. – advocating a more professionally oriented education which would give the individual the best professional qualifications. At the same time, the professional qualifications must be completed by a development of culture sufficient not only to enable the individual to adapt himself constantly to the rapid changes in his profession and the society, but also to enable him to participate fully in a society of "people's government" based on a "civilization of labor . . . in which each individual is participating in both the production and the consumption of all the goods."

Confronted with these new elements, education in Europe has for a long time remained static in its methods and structures, which has made the expression "education in crisis" hit the headlines.

Over the last ten years, ministerial committees charged with examination and elaboration of projects for reform have multiplied; in professorial and student circles, as well as in the nation in general, stands are taken in favor of or against proposed reforms, the necessity for which is denied by no one. European and Atlantic organizations with economic responsibilities, such as the OECD, have studied the problem and have certainly contributed to the development of the theory that education is an essential element for economic and social development. Moreover, education has been the object of passionate political and ideological debates in which too often the projects for reform have been judged in terms of the past rather than in terms of the future.

Meanwhile education has gone through a first quantitative revolution posing serious material and financial problems to the students, professors, and governmental bodies. In less than fifteen years (1955-1970) the student population will approximately have doubled.

One should note that this expansion of European higher education comes nearly forty years after a similar expansion in the United States, while early in this century there was no important difference between the number of graduates of higher education on the two continents. "While in the United States the number of graduates quintupled between 1919 and 1935, in the same period the number of university students was halved in Germany, and in France, Holland, England, and Italy it increased in proportion varying from only fifteen to sixty percent."[1]

The object of our study then is to analyse the way in which European governments and power groups are coping with the modernization of higher education, and therefore we present, in the first part, the factors which have brought about expansion of higher education and its crisis. Next, we present an analysis of the various power groups with reference to the change in the nature of the university. This brings us to consider extensively the democratization of education, giving us a notion of the economic, social, and political attitudes which guide the planning approach to the development of education in its financial aspects. In the last instance, we take into consideration the effects of the development of education on the European student society in which a constant evolution is to be noted, reflecting the more general opening up of the academic community to the world at large.

University Expansion

To adapt the university to the economic and social conditions of the contemporary world, i.e., the needs of the economy and democratization, is the principle which is accepted virtually unanimously throughout Europe. It was laid down at the close of the Second World War by, among others, the Langevin-Wallon French ministerial commission on education.[a] But the difficulties in putting these principles into practice are enormous, as we shall see, and

---

[a]See chapter 2. In fact, the same principle dates back in France at least to the close of the First World War with "Les Compagnons de l'Université Nouvelle."

do not fail to nourish passionate discussions and conflicts between the various powers involved in higher education.

If Europe can indeed claim to have the oldest institutions of higher learning in the world, still offering a model to those set up in the newer countries, and if it inherited beautiful traditions, it has, also, greater difficulties than others in proceeding to the necessary modernization.

Tradition is a crushing and ambiguous force and provokes crises of conscience among those who uphold it — the academic community which remains largely closed to the outsider. Educators who, as the "technicians of education" preside over the destiny of the university, train and recuit each other. From this stems the fact that:

At the scale of successive generations, two, three centuries of history seem amazingly short; only five to six generations of teachers seperate us from the colleges of the Ancient Regime, and the generation that constitutes itself today will be but renewed at the approach of the year 2000. From which stems the force of tradition and the delay of education behind the state of society.[2]

Without any doubt, the teachers want to participate directly in progress, but they want just as much, or even more, to guard traditions which have proved successful. "Each of these two opposed tendencies is in turn dominated and dominating. Thus are explained the fragmentary measures, the tentative procedures, and the oscillations which for almost 200 years have marked the history of education."[3]

Perhaps events of exceptional vigor had to take place to modify the respective influences of these tendencies. Such events are now happening in Europe, with the profound changes that the society is undergoing and the "explosion scolaire," the extraordinary increase in the number of students enrolling in the university which must, as stated by one of their more important organizations — l'Union nationale des etudiants de France (National union of France's students), "take charge also of the professional training of all higher professionals of the country and not only of the future professors and researchers for whom the degrees have been and still are provided. Because the vocation of the university has changed, a tremendous effort of reorganization at all levels and all cycles of study is required."

The complexity of the reasons that brought about the expansion in the enrollment of students at the universities is such that it is very hazardous to try to name and analyse all of them. But a few observations have to be made. The increase at the level of higher education (see Tables 1-1, 1-2, 1-3, 1-4, and 1-5) which started to be obvious from the early 1950's onwards is not due to the increase of the birth rate which appeared in Europe at the close of the Second World War. The expansion was stimulated by a profound change of the "social demand" for prolonged education, a modification of the "behavior" of families toward secondary and higher education. First middle-class families, then lower-class families tended to model their customs after those of the higher classes. As Raymond Poignant remarked, "This element alone led to a doubling

Table 1-1

Federal Republic of Germany and West
Berlin: Increase in the Number of
Students (in thousands) [a]

| | 1950-51 | 1960-61 | Variations 51-61 | | 1963-64 | Forecast[c] 1970 |
			Full Figure	Index 61 basis 100 in 1951		
Universities and Technical schools	111.3[b]	184.5	+ 72.2	166	219.1	232.2
Pedagogic institutes	11.4[b]	33.1	+ 21.7	290	44	
TOTAL	122.7[b]	217.6	+ 94.9	177	263.1	

[a]Source: Statistiches Bundesamt. Raymond Poignant, "L'enseignement dans les pays du Marche Commun," Paris, 1966. Chart Annexe I, p. 297.

[b]The Sarre not included.

[c]Wissenschaftsrat.

Table 1-2

The Netherlands: Increase in the Number of Students [a]

1920-21	1937-38	1947-48	1955-56	1963-64[b]	1970-71
8,552	12,505	25,955	29,642	52,400	82,000

[a]Source: Publication of Central Bureau of Statistics, Holland (La Haye) and the Ministry of Education and Science, Documentation Service, Docinform 162.

[b]Raymond Poignant, "L'Enseignement dans les pays du Marche Commun," Paris, 1966, Chart Annexe VI, pp. 306-307.

Table 1-3

Belgium: Increase in the Number of
Students [a]

Years	Basic Population (age group 17, 18, 19, and 20)	Belgian students beginning higher studies[b]	% of new students in relation to the basic population	Total population of higher education[b]	% of new students to the total number of students
1948-49	131,226	4,032	3.07	17,764	22.70
1952-53[c]	120,063	4,646	3.87	20,260	22.93
1957-58	115,491	5,997	5.19	24,983	24.00
1959-60	99,609	6,321	6.35	26,836	23.55
1960-61	99,984	6,713	6.71	28,106	23.88
1962-63[c]	117,549	8,099	6.89	32,098	25.23
1970	140,375	12,415	8.84	46,550	26.67

[a]Source: "Counseil National de la Politique Scientifique," Brussels, "Rapport sur l'expansion et l'adaption de L'enseignement superieur de niveau universitaire," 23 March 1964, page 27, Table 8.

[b]Students of Higher Commercial Institutes (evening courses) are not included.

[c]Real figures.

of the number of students of the 'lycees' from 1947 to 1957, even before the demographic boom had reached the classes of the 'sixième' (first class of secondary school in France).[4]

This increase in the number of students, even without an increase in the size of the age group, produced a mushrooming effect on enrollments at all levels. The French publication, "L'Explosion Scolaire," pointed out that, "In 1900, for an average of 800,000 annual births, there were six million pupils in all types of schools . . . In 1970, educational enrollment will reach the figure of eleven million from a birthrate essentially the same as that of 1900 . . . "[5]

As a matter of fact, in France, the increase of 73 percent in the number of students enrolling in the university between 1951 and 1961 is explained by factors other than demography. One of the factors of expansion is a policy of "economic" democratization on the part of the authorities (central government, university, private foundations) limited to the granting of financial aid to needy students in the form of scholarships and long-term loans free of interest for

Table 1-4

France: Increase in the Number of Students (in thousands) [a]

	1951-52			1961-62			Variations 52-62		1963-64		
	Public	Private	Total	Publ.	Priv.	Totl.	Full Fig.	Index' 61 Basis 100 in 1951	Publ.	Priv.	Totl.
Public & private faculties	137	3.7[b]	140.7	245	7[c]	252	+111.3	179	326	8[c]	334
Other private & public Superior schools	14.8	6.3	21.1	19	11	30	+ 1.9	140	26	12	38
Total	151.8	10	161.8	264	18.6	282	+120.2	174	352	20	372

[a] Source: Statistiques du Ministere de l'Education Nationale ("Informations statistiques" et publications du B.U.S.)

[b] The number of students of the private faculties not included in the one of the public faculties.

[c] Estimation of the number of students of the various schools not enrolled in the university institutions.

Table 1-5

Italy: Increase in the Number of
Students (in thousands) [a]

| | 1938-39 | 1952-53 | 1962-63 | Variations 53-63 | | 1964-65 |
				Full Figure	Index '63 basis 100 in 1953	
Higher Education	236	224	273	+49	122	350

[a]Sources: Statistiques Scolaires et Universitaires. Raymond Poignant, "L'Enseignement dans les pays du Marche Commun," Paris, 1966. Chart Annexe IV, pp. 302-303.

which factors such as age, financial situation of the family, and type of studies are taken into consideration. With regard to the latter, one might reasonably expect that this policy directs the student to a particular type of study for which most of the financial aid is reserved and thus might interfere with the student's desires.

One should note that it was only in 1958 that France proceeded to a reform of its scholarship granting system. As for the Netherlands, the sums available for government grants have sharply risen. In 1950, only 2,370,000 guilders was spent; by 1960 they amounted to 20,160,000 guilders and by 1964 to 48,778,190, of which 27,012,205 is given as grants and 21,765,985 as interest-free loans. According to law, the individual amount may not exceed 3,400 guilders, of which 200 is intended to cover tuition fees. Today, about 35 percent of the students receive financial aid of some kind.[6]

In Belgium, by the law of March 19, 1954, the "Fonds National des Etudes" is entrusted with the granting of financial aid to needy and gifted students. Since the academic year 1957-58, the number of scholarships granted by the Foundation to first-year students increased from 1,824 to 3,807 and their total amount from 26,946,900 to 65,384,500 Belgian Francs.

The total amount of scholarships for university studies granted by the Foundation amounts to 227,990,000 Belgian Francs for the academic year 1962-63. (see Table 1-7). It was 197,554,800 for the academic year 1955-56.[7]

A third factor which accounts for the expansion of higher education in Europe are the various governmental and university measures to open the university by changing the admission requirements: a burning and controversial subject in the teaching community, particularly regarding the type of study the student should have received in secondary school. (Greek and Latin).

Traditionally, the individual who wants to enroll at the university must hold the degree conferred upon him at the completion of secondary school studies

Table 1-6

Universities and Assimilated Institutions
in the Common Market Countries[a]

Countries	Universities Number	Actuals	Similar Establishments Number	Actuals
1. Federal Republic of Germany	18	209,300 (1964-1965)	8 "Technische Hochschulen"[b] 5 "Spezial Hochschulen"[c] 17 College of Theology	58,500 4,800 2,600
2. Belgium	4[d]	30,431 (1962-1963)	16 specialized institutions[e]	4,830
3. France	19	326,300 (1963-1964)	2 applied science institutes (Lyon, Toulouse) 10 high institutions and high academies[f]	h 8,000[g]
4. Italy	27 public 4 private	180,500 (1962-1963) 22,000 (1960)	2 University Institutes 4 special institutes 6 private institutes of "magistero" 4 private institutes of physical education	7,300 7,500 7,500 1,500 (1962-63)
5. Holland	6[i]	47,063 (1962)	5 Colleges	h

[a]Source: Raymond Poignant, "L'Enseignement dans les pays du Marche Commun," Paris, 1966.

[b]Technical universities.

[c]Specialized colleges.

[d]State university of Gand and Liege, Free University of Brussels, Catholic University of Louvain.

[e]The Belgian law of April 9, 1965 divides in this category: The university centers of Antwerp and Mons; the four university faculties of Brussels, Namur, Antwerp and Mons; the four superior institutions (specialized); the six colleges of Commerce.

[f]Institutions depending on the Direction of Higher Education, such as the "College de France," "Ecoles Normales Superieures," "le Museum d'histoire naturelle," "l'Ecole de Chartres," etc.

[g]Students not enrolled in other respects in the public faculties (estimation).

[h]Actuals included in the total of the universities.

[i]Three state universities (Leyde, Gronigue, Utrecht), municipal University of Amsterdam and the free universities of Amsterdam (Calvinist) and Nimegue (Catholic).

Table 1-7

Distribution of Newly Enrolled Students Benefiting and Not Benefiting from Grants, per Enlarged Socio-Professional Category (academic year 1962-63)[a]

Socio-professional categories[b]	Scholarship holders	%	Without Scholarship	%
A. Workers	711	80.8	169	19.2
B. Subordinate employees, retailers and artisans (without staff or of 5 persons)	1,021	62.3	617	37.7
C. Average professionals, teachers, professors of lower education	954	58.2	970	41.8
D. Professors of higher education and higher professionals	225	21.4	826	78.6
E. Chiefs of Enterprise (5 to 49 persons) and holder of free profession	197	17.2	948	82.8
F. Chiefs of Enterprise (50 persons and more), professors of university and magistrates	20	6.4	394	93.6
G. Agriculturists	283	74.1	99	25.9
Total	3,708	100.0	4,148	100.0
Percentage	47.2	-	52.8	-

[a]Source: Conseil National de la Politique Scientifique, Brussels. Rapport sur l'expansion et l'adaptation de l'Enseignement superieur de niveau universitaire, 23 1964, p. 74.

[b]Student organizations in Europe claim the need for a "salaire universitaire" (study salary) because they consider that the student, the intellectual worker, conditions in part the future economic and social expansion of the community and that, for this reason, one can talk of "the differing productivity of student work" (Dossiers du Mouvement des Etudiants belges d'espression francaise — 2nd edition, No. 3, p. 12). See also Chapter 4.

(Baccalaureat in France, Abitur in Germany, Diplôme des Humanités in Belgium and Luxemburg, Maturita (classica, scientifica) in Italy, final certificate of the Gymnasium or Hogere Burgersschool [H.B.S.] in the Netherlands.

In the countries of the Common Market the degree of final secondary school studies is sufficient for entrance into the university. This system excludes as such any "numerus clausus" or quota system. It is then the number of secondary school graduates which determines the number of university students, and thus the size of the universities. In the Federal Republic of Germany and in France, the "polyvalence" of the secondary school degree is, in principle, total, and permits enrollment in any faculty. In fact, as observes Raymond Poignant, the studies show that secondary school programs, in terms of the "section" (classic, modern, science, etc.) pre-orient the student towards certain types of higher education. In Belgium, by virtue of the law of June 8, 1964, this same "polyvalence" is granted. Here one should note that before this law only the classic (Greek and Latin) section of secondary school permitted entrance into any faculty, whereas from the science section students were directed toward the Faculty of Science, and from the economic section students could only pursue higher studies in commercial sciences. Statistics then proved that children coming from the highest social levels enrolled in the classical section, whereas the children coming from lower social classes formed over 90 percent of the students in the economic section and could never attend those faculties offering professional training of highest prestige (law, medicine, pharmacy, letters and philosophy, engineering, etc).

In the Netherlands, the old Belgian system remains in effect, and each section of the secondary school corresponds to a section in the university.

Only in France and Belgium is there a "selective" system of entrance: for the famous "Grandes Ecoles" and business schools in France, on the basis of a competitive entrance examination; and in Belgium, with respect to the faculties and schools of applied sciences, by a noncompetitive entrance examination.

Furthermore, only recently does there exist in the Common Market countries what is called "the second way" (Zweite Bildungsweg) for entrance into the university. It is open to graduates of technical secondary schools, and anyone who wishes to do so can obtain the equivalent of secondary school studies by taking the "special examinations" which he prepares on his own.

In fact, according to the Robbins' Report, in Western Europe, with the exception − to a certain extent − of Great Britain, higher education has benefited little from such measures.[8]

The needs of the economy, as they orient public school policy, have been a stimulating factor for expansion of higher education, under the forms which we described previously. By the creation of new institutions of higher learning, in parts of the country deprived of any such institution until then, they opened up new possibilities to adolescents for whom the distance from the school often constituted an obstacle to his decision to pursue higher studies. Whereas in France this decentralization process was concerned until recently mainly with secondary technical schools, in Belgium, under the law of April 9, 1965, new private faculties (University of Brussels, Catholic University of Louvin) and public faculties (University of Ghent and Liege) — faculties of the sciences, applied economics, pedagogy, and school for interpreters — have been or will be opened for the sake of decentralization. But no studies have so far been conducted as to the influence these new institutions will have on the enrollment of students of the regions concerned. In Holland, in view of the government's industrialization policy, priority has been given to higher technical education. On the basis of the recommendations of two commissions set up for the study of the problems of higher technical education, the Delft Technological University was greatly extended and renovated. In 1956, a second technological university comprising three branches of study — mechanical, technical, and chemical engineering — was established in Eindhoven (1,342 students, 1961-62). As for Germany, new universities were or are on the point of being opened — the University of Bremen and the University in Bochum (Ruhr).

A fifth and last factor which to us seems to have been of significance with respect to the increase in the number of students over the last twenty years in Europe, is the greater enrollment of female students. This phenomenon could be explained by the fact that many professions, previously reserved to male graduates, are now being opened to women. Most of the female students are to be found in schools preparing for the teaching profession. Planners are more and more interested in knowing what proportion of women is practicing a profession a few years after graduation, as this knowledge could be of great importance in evaluating the future supply of graduates.

Without any doubt, this "quantitative revolution" has brought about material problems with regard to the necessary investments, space, and teaching staffs. Further, it has affected the structure of higher education in Europe. The significance of the increase can only be understood when one observes that the legal structures of university education remain largely the same as those of the 19th century, when the university was almost totally composed of students coming from higher social classes. Moreover, when new universities were built, and there were few, the old university was the model.

As we have already observed, it is the access of new social strata to university education which has brought about the increase in the number of students since the last World War. If one cannot reasonably maintain that talent and intelligence of individuals vary according to the social class to which they belong, it is certainly true that children are exposed to the influence of the milieu to which they belong and, as such, an important role is played in their early education by the culture of social class.

However, the academic authorities elaborate the programs of study according to the way it was done early this century and impose them upon the students who have no way of discussing them, but according to which they will have to pass exams which in their turn will classify them as good or bad. One realizes, then, the importance of the criteria according to which these programs are elaborated.

One of these criteria is the concept that children coming from different social and geographic milieu are "interchangeable," that is, that intelligence is distributed at the moment of birth without any distinction of class, and that all the children of any class have the same chance to acquire knowledge up to the highest level.

Students then attend a university which in its basic organization is still that of the last century; and, as such, was created for an elite which received there the scientific instruction necessary to perform an independent profession or to be oriented toward research. But a great number of students who attend a university today are not asking these goals of their university education. Few are interested in research; many are asking from their higher education that it grant them the possibility of practicing a profession; others are demanding that the degrees conferred upon them enable them to compete for civil service jobs. Thus there exists a tremendous cultural gap between the traditions that the university is upholding and the type of schooling many students are demanding. Hence, the crisis.

A cause and expression of this crisis at the same time is the relatively high percentage of failures at the examinations and the high number of students lagging behind in comparison with the normal cycles of study (see Table 1-8). In his opening speech for the academic year 1963, Mr. Bouckaert, Rector of the University of Ghent (Belgium) cited the figure of 55 percent of failures in the first year for the whole of the university during the academic year 1958-59.[9] As for the University of Brussels (private), if one takes into consideration only the students from the second year and beyond, one finds that, in 1963-64, only 43.2 percent pursued their studies without any delay.[10]

Table 1-8

Rate of Success in Higher Education in
the Common Market Countries

Country	Number admitted in % of age group	Number of graduates in % of age group	Rate of Success
West Germany[a]	4.2 (1957-58)	2.5 (1963)	60%
France[b]	6.7 (1956-57)	3.8 (1960-1961)	57%
Belgium[c]	- - - -	- - - -	60%
Italy	4.4 (1954-55)	2.8 (1958-1959)	63%
Holland	3.4 (1956-57)	2.0 (1962-1963)	58%

[a]Universities only.

[b]Universities and "Grandes Ecoles".

[c]Enseignment Normal moyen et ecoles d'ingenieurs-techniciens seulement.

Table 1-9

Number of Years Behind Schedule of
Second Year and Beyond Belgian Students at the Free University of Brussels
(doctorate and various specialties excluded)

Year of Delay	0	1	2	3	4	5	6	+6
No.	1,605	1,269	372	140	77	63	36	117
%	43.2	34.2	10.0	3.8	2.1	1.7	1.0	3.1

In France, with respect to faculties, one can reasonably claim that the 57 percent success rate is too high, as this percentage includes the famous "Grandes Ecoles" where success rates amount up to 99.9 or 100 percent. The 60 percent given for Belgium accounts only for the success rate in the "Enseignement Normal Moyen" (preparing teachers for the first three years of secondary education) and engineers'-technicians' schools. Table 1-9, with regard to the Brussels University, shows the extent students' failures are important at the university. For the sake of comparison, Table 1-10 shows the rate of success in the British universities, where entrance is based on a severe selection procedure.

Supported by this relatively high success rate in British universities, some continental educators advocate the introduction of a selection system in which they see the salvation of the quality of higher education. Opposition on the part of the students and professors on this point is strong and would certainly provoke strikes and marches on their part, as it is considered an attempt to limit freedom of access to the university, a principle which has been upheld for centuries. The fear is that one will select in terms of the room and professors available, rather than in terms of intelligence criteria which, in their turn, will create lively tensions on all levels if considered.

Another cause and effect of the crisis is the well-known incapacity of university graduates to adapt themselves to the tasks which society is de-manding, notably in industry, which tends to prove that university structure and curriculum content are far from adapted to the economic and social conditions of society.

"Let's speak in figures," says Mr. P. Bochet, member of the Board of Directors of the Centre des Jeunes Patrons in Paris. "Presently . . . the adaptation of an engineer to the life of the company takes about one year. It is only after this period that the man is integrated and that he attains his optimum efficiency. Well, the cost of this year, social benefits included (social security, pension, vacations, etc.), corresponds to that of three to four years of higher

Table 1-10

Rate of Success in the British Universities (1960-1961)[a]

Subject	Success in the course of normal term %	Success after a longer duration %	Still continuing %	Failures %
Arts and Social sciences	86.3	-	2.1	11.9
Pure sciences	82.9	-	2.3	14.7
Applied sciences	72.5	-	7.5	20.8
Agriculture	83.4	-	4.4	14.2
Medicine & Dentistry	57.2	30	2.8	10.0
Veterinary Medicine	56.9	25.9	2.7	15.0

[a]Source: Report of the University's Grants Committee for 1960-61, as taken from Raymond Poignant, "L'enseignement dans les pays du Marche Commun," Paris, 1966, p. 195, Chart No. 68.

education. This means that every effort which is undertaken to permit a more rapid adaptation of a man to a company will be, speaking in economic terms . . . profitable for the community, even if it implies a lengthening of his studies." As to the reasons for this inadaptation, he cites those which are inherent to the inadaptability of character, e.g., bad orientation; those which are due to the inadaptability of knowledge, e.g., bad training or bad curriculum; and those which are due to the gap which exists between the world of studies and the life of the companies, e.g., social confinement.

To these accusations, Professor Jean Frenkel, of the Faculty of Science at the University of Strasbourg, would reply, "The inadaptation of higher education stems from the fact that one presently asks it to accomplish a task which is not its own and for which it is not equipped: mass education destined to form medium professionals."

Another aspect of crisis stems from the limited choice that secondary school graduates find in "real" higher education systems, that is, those to which a very high cultural and social prestige is attached — the traditional universities. It is indeed the case that in Europe *the* higher education is received in the traditional university and, for France, in the "Grandes Ecoles," but that in the latter the number of students is limited. The very fact that earlier in this study we had to distinguish between university and assimilated institutions and nonuniversity institutions (although they counted as higher educational institutes) demonstrates the distinctions one is bound to make between a student attending the university and the one who attends a technical institution. The families know it, the students know it, the society stimulating the "image" knows it, and thus, naturally, even to the extent of not directly considering his own future financial interest, the student will direct himself toward the university. Eventually, he may change his initial choice, but then only as the result of a failure, which makes Professor Capelle say: "We are all the failures of something." Orientation through failure!

The nature of the crisis and its extent reach such disastrous peaks for the student, psychologically affected by his failures, the economy, the university, and the society as a whole, that reforms are mandatory, deep reforms to keep Europe's economy, served by highly qualified personnel, on its path of expansion and in competition with the other countries of the world.

Raymond Poignant one of France's educational planning experts, finds, after a five year fact-finding study in cooperation with the various governments, that Europe is losing the race for graduates, and insists that "the key to the problem of increasing the rhythm of training of higher professionals" is to be found in democratization at the secondary school level.

University Structures

Federal Republic of Germany

In the Federal Republic of Germany, the institutions of higher education (Hochschulen) comprise the universities (Universitäten), the Technical High Schools (Technische Hochschulen), a small number of other institutions (Spezial Hochschulen) which have only limited fields of teaching and research, and schools of theology.

The traditions established by Wilhelm von Humboldt — founder of the University of Berlin in 1810 — have for the most part been maintained, but today one can observe slight changes. Humboldt's doctrine created an intimate link between research and teaching exercised in complete personal freedom, one of the fundamental exigencies of the philosophy of German idealism, making the pursuit of knowledge the essential task of the professor, whose teaching had to be based upon his research. As for the student, he had to train himself by participating directly in the evolution of scientific knowledge. Of course this unity of research and teaching has never been completely realized, a fact which makes Professor Dahrendorf observe:

The Berlin tradition is indeed theoretical from at least three points of view: it privileges research over teaching and didactic problems; it privileges science over its application in the professions for which the university prepares; and in research itself it privileges the reflective and philosophical element over the experimental one.[11]

This academic freedom, as it developed in the 19th century, defines today not only the work of the professor but also of the student, who is free with regard to the choice of a university and who can in the course of studies freely change from one university to another. Moreover, the student is responsible for the planning of his studies, and is free to decide when he will present himself for the examinations. The German system organizes only final examinations in most branches of study (Abschlussesamen), but for medicine and dentistry there exists a preliminary examination (Voresamen).

However, the student is in fact quite limited in the exercise of this freedom because of professional requirements. Indeed, many university courses lead to state examinations. In its 1960 report the Council for Arts and Science (Wissenschaftsrat) points out:

There is constant tension and friction between the idealist educational philosophy of German universities and the practical purpose which the state expects them to fulfill as institutions for the training of priests, teachers, physicians, judges, and administrators . . . The state administration in Germany aims at attaining a monopoly in education and endeavors to bring about a uniform education of the experts it requires. It has consequently narrowed the principle of freedom in academic studies by its examination regulations. The tension thus created still exists today.

And the British Robbins' Report states, "It was this conflict between the needs of the nation and the traditional view that only arts and science in their pure forms were appropriate for university study that led to the foundation of the technical high schools."[1 2]

These technical high schools — which had been preceded by the Mining Schools of Berlin (1699), Freiburg/Saxe (1765), and Clausthal (1775), took for a model the Ecole Polytechnique de Paris (1794)[b] and adapted it to the needs of industrialization. The technical high schools at first possessed neither the appearance nor the stature of the universities. But, as in the second part of the 19th century the increasing specialization of the old universities and the increasing general training of the technical schools approached one another, the latter were granted the stature of the universities. Because of the nature of the subjects taught, as well as their later founding, the technical schools have remained free from the university tradition and students are expected to conform to such things as attendance requirements.

The duration of studies is at least four to five years (letters, sciences, theology). In medicine the studies take eleven semesters and a practical training period of one-and-a-half years. Although the Standing Conference of the Education Ministers of the Länder[c] has laid down the minimum number of semesters to precede the final examinations, it appears that in general the time

---

[b]Ecole Polytechnique de Paris (1794), restricted and specialized institution of higher learning which does not have any relation with the other IHL, and whose purpose was, as laid down by the 'Convention': "a instruire et a former pour les ecoles d'application des grands services publics, civils et militaires des eleves possedant des connaissances scientifiques etendues."

[c]The Länder governments, sovereign in education, have established the Standing Conference of Ministers of Education in order to achieve uniformity and agreement on essential matters of mutual interest.

needed for a student to complete his studies is more than the suggested minimum, which poses the question of the duration and "efficiency" of studies. It should be noted that the students who receive a public award are expected to complete their studies within the required period of time.

The Council for Arts and Science, as well as the Standing Conference of Education Ministers, has recommended that traditional teaching by lectures and formal demonstrations should be completed by seminars, which would require a greater number of professors than exists today in most institutions. It would also mean a closer control of the student's studies.

Belgium

Belgian higher education consists of four universities (two state universities, Ghent and Liege; two private universities, Louvain (Catholic) and Brussels (libre-examen), and sixteen specialized institutions of university rank (agronomy, veterinary, medicine, applied science, commerce). All have complete independence in matters of academic policy and are largely autonomous except for some administrative control by the Higher Education and Scientific Department in the Ministry of National Education and Culture.

The organization of the Belgian universities is based upon division into six faculties: philosophy and letters, law, science, medicine, applied science, and social science.

University studies are organized at three levels. The first constitutes a means of selecting the students, but appears to us to become of less selective significance from the moment there is the "maturity" examination upon leaving the secondary school and new requirements for entrance into the university: the "candidature" requires two years of study and two examinations in letters philosophy and science; three years of study and three examinations in medicine and natural sciences. The "license" can be obtained after two more years of study and two more examinations. The "doctorat" is obtained after at least one more year of study in letters and science, and in these branches of study the obtaining of the doctorate requires the presentation of a thesis; but the doctorate in law and medicine does not require a thesis and constitutes the final ordinary diploma for these studies. The duration of studies is presented in Table 1-11.

These degrees are conferred either as "legal" degrees (diplôme legal) or "scientific" degrees (diplôme scientifique); the latter are conferred by the universities only to those students who did not at the start of their studies fulfill the standard academic requirements (of interest in particular to foreign students). These candidates can, if they wish, 'legalize' their position by sitting for an examination with the National Board (Jury Central). The 'legal' degrees confer upon the holder the right to exercise a profession which is organized by

Table 1-11

Belgium: Duration of Studies[a]

Branch of Study	License No. of Years	Doctorate No. of Years
Law	-	5
Economic, political, social science	4	5
Psychology, pedagogy	4	5
Philosophy and Letters	4	5
Sciences	4	5
Medicine	-	7
Pharmacy	5	-
Dentistry	5	-
Civil engineer	5	-
Agronomy (engineer)	5	-

[a]Source: Raymond Poignant, "L'enseigne-ment dans les pays du Marche Commun," Paris, 1966, p. 167.

law. It should be pointed out that the National Board cannot confer a doctorate in science, medicine, or philosophy.

The schedule of the students varies from faculty to faculty and becomes shorter as the studies go toward the final examinations. At the start, in the "candidature" which still has some general courses, they occupy about twenty hours per week.

As in the Netherlands and Germany, or for that matter anywhere else in Western Europe, the student is free to organize his work, free to attend classes or not. The methods of teaching, particularly in the literary branches of study, are still based on the scholastic tradition and the custom of lecturing ex cathedra. In Belgium these are also published as "cours polycopie" which is a way to keep the student out of already overcrowded amphitheatres since he can buy the professor's lectures, even corrected by the latter.

The Netherlands

Higher education in the Netherlands comprises six universities and five specialist institutes of university rank in which teaching and research are concentrated on one field (technological sciences, agricultural sciences, economics) and which can lead to a doctorate.

The universities comprise five to seven faculties. Three of these universities are state institutions (Leyden, Groningen, and Utrecht). The University of Amsterdam is a municipal institution, the Free University of Amsterdam (Reformed) and the University of Nijmegen (Catholic); these universities have at least the faculties of theology, medicine, mathematics and physics, law, letters and philosophy. Moreover the University of Utrecht has a faculty of veterinary medicine; the University of Groningen and the Free University of Amsterdam have faculties of economics. The University of Amsterdam (municipal) is completed by a faculty of economic sciences and a faculty of political and social sciences. Finally, dentistry is taught at the faculties of medicine of the universities of Groningen and Utrecht.

Certain studies, however, are considered to have to deal with various faculties and therefore intermediary sections called "interfaculties" (inter-faculteiten) have been created. Psychology and pedagogy constitute an interfaculty bringing together medicine and letters; sociology is taught in an interfaculty uniting law, letters, and economic sciences.

Strongly influenced by the German tradition, the Dutch university developed over the last century according to the conception of the idealist philosophy of the early 19th century to which it still owes its fundamental characteristics, among which is the great autonomy of the professors. However, the state universities are state controlled and their administration is a branch of the civil service. According to the Robbins' Report this has lead to a diarchy within the universities with the academic and administrative staffs sometimes scarcely on speaking terms. There was little sense of corporate unity and even some appearance of inertia, since no single person or office had responsibility for leadership. "But now that university departments are growing, both in the number of their students and of their staff, the professors are virtually being compelled to adapt themselves to some type of organization and coordination — if only to ensure the continued satisfactory functioning of their own departments." Mr. Vander Wilk, of the University of Leyden, pointed out to us that this adaptation of the professor is sometimes painful, and perhaps many years will be needed to come to a satisfactory situation in this respect.

The length of courses of study up to the final examination is indicated in Table 1-12. Notice the exceptionally long period of study.

In all the faculties examinations are organized at two levels: The candidature (tentamen) which is taken by the student at the moment of his choice. Indeed, there are no examination sessions as such, but the professor indicates that he will hold "tentamen" at dates which he believes opportune, generally at the end of a quarter. This examination is taken after two to three years of study. The second is the final examination which has various names, i.e., Doctorandus, master for law students, degree "arts" in medicine; "apotheker" in pharmacy, engineer in

Table 1-12

The Netherlands: Duration of Studies[a]

Branches of Study	Normal Duration
Theology	4 years
Law	5 years
Medicine	7 to 8 years
Dentistry	6 to 7 years
Sciences	6 to 7 years
Letters	5 to 6 years
Economic sciences	5 to 6 years
Social sciences	5 to 6 years
Veterinary medicine	6 years
Technology	6 years
Agronomy	5 to 6 years

[a]Source: Raymond Poignant, "L'enseignement dans les pays du Marche Commun,"
Paris, 1966, p. 171.

technology. For this examination the student informs the professor that he is
ready and they settle on a date for the examination.

The doctorate (Doctoraal) is conferred on Doctorandi and "ingenieurs" after
publication of a thesis approved by any professor prepared to sponsor it.

Content of courses: The concept of "course" does not exist in traditional
higher education. From the time the student enters the university, he should be
prepared to work independently and participate in original work. Recently,
however, many have opposed this procedure because they feel that the average
student's needs are neglected. Some professors feel that the first years in the
university should be dedicated to teaching the student how to work; and
Dr. Woltjer, adviser to the Dutch Ministry of Education, comes out strongly in
favor of a less abrupt transition from the conditions of work in the secondary
school to those in the university. It seems that the universities deal with this

problem by exercising a closer control of the work of the student, especially in the early years, "and by aiming to eliminate genuinely unsuitable students within their first university year," reports the Robbins Committee.[13]

Italy

Higher education in Italy comprises twenty-seven public universities and four private universities; two university institutes; four specialized institutes; six private institutes "magistero" or "teacher colleges" training secondary school teachers, and four institutes (private) of physical education.

The Italian universities are composed of a great number of faculties: law, philosophy and letters, political sciences, medicine, technology, mathematics, physics, natural sciences, veterinary medicine, agriculture, economics, architecture, "magistero" (special faculties for teacher training).

Programs of study in the various majors are very rigidly organized. Intermediate examinations are held by each faculty; in most cases these examinations must be taken at the end of each academic year. A program of study usually takes four years. A doctorate in engineering and architecture may be taken after five years, one in medicine after six years. Almost all programs of study are completed by the obtaining of the "Laurea" (licence). Academic degrees conferred by private universities are recognized and considered equal to those conferred by the state universities. There exists in Italy no systematic training for scientific research. The training of researchers is taken care of by the training of the university "cadres" themselves through assistantships.

Transfer from one university to another or a change in majors is not common, but may take place with special permission of the university president. Courses in general education are not required.

The faculties which can be created, admission requirements, the so-called fundamental teachings, and the degrees are organized by the state. The interior organization of the faculties, on the other hand, is organized by the statute that each university gives itself and is the expression of the autonomy of the universities.

France

Higher education in France comprises nineteen universities, two institutes of applied sciences, ten institutes and "grandes ecoles," and nine private faculties or group of faculties (with only 8,000 students).

Public education in France is highly centralized, but nevertheless very complex. A strong influence on the organization and administration of education is exercised by the National Assembly which approves all subsidies and decides on the establishment of new institutions and their functions, and on the size of the teaching and administrative staffs. The Ministry executes the decisions made by the National Assembly; in addition it possesses extensive authority and powers of its own, e.g., appointment of teachers and the introduction of various examination regulations.

The universities are organized on the basis of faculties (humanities, law, pure sciences, medicine and pharmacy.) The faculties are the real basis of French higher education in the university which has little freedom structurally. For example, economic sciences had to develop in the faculty of law, and the social sciences under the faculty of letters. Complaints on the part of the professors and students in these fields that this structure does not enable their branch of studies to develop fully are often heard.

Political Forces and General Structural Problems

When, around the year 1750, the "Privatdozent" Immanuel Kant started his career at the University of Konisberg, it was well understood that his task was not to expose his personal ideas but to interpret "Compendia," i.e., textbooks, representing the authoritative source for professors and students alike. And even if Fichte later praised Kant for liberating himself from the textbooks, they remained the foundation and the real content of his too many courses. Zedlitz, the minister to whom Kant dedicated his "Critique of Pure Reason," decreed in 1778 that: "The most vicious Compendium is still better than no Compendium at all. The professors can, if they have that much sagacity, improve their authors, but one must in any case put an end to the lectures based on plain notes . . . " That was what academic freedom was like in the 18th century, and not only in Prussia.

With the wave of liberalism of the 19th century, the academic community found greater freedom, as characterized by the liberal reforms introduced at the University of Berlin. Professors still remained largely responsible to highly centralized bureaucracies, as in France, but they could reinforce their independence of teaching and research, while the pressures from the outside world were rather easily dealt with.

But with the present crisis in higher education and the recent concept that education is essential to the national economic and social development, new forces intend to play a role in the reorganization of the European educational system.

All claim reforms are mandatory. Their reasons: "adaptation," Government, business, industry and university administrations; students and professors – and "democratization." But it is with regard to the spirit, the form and the way in which these reforms will be carried out that opposition between forces arises, resulting in short-lived alliances. The essential vice of all the reforms is that they are made by diplomatic methods, by the way of negotiations from power to power, with the subtle play of alliances and oppositions . . . as one used to draft in former times the motions in the radical (party) congress.

With respect to the tremendous increase in the number of students, the crisis, and the subsequent policy of academic authorities (bureaucracy), government, and the business world, Professor Maurice Duverger, from the University of Paris, denounces "university malthusianism," based upon the idea that quality of education necessarily suffers from the quantity of students. But, says Duverger, that simply poses the problem of more professors. As for "government's malthusianism," it is stimulated by the high rate of failures, as a result of which government hesitates to proceed with the necessary investments. "I claim," says Duverger, "that anyone who has spent a couple of years at the university has not lost his time." And he says of "business world malthusianism":

At the Commission of the Eighteen (entrusted with the preparation of reforms of higher education) it was, it seems, the representatives of the private companies who insisted upon the necessity to place barriers at the entrance to higher education so as to admit only the most brilliant individuals; as for the others, they should enter as fast as possible into the companies and be given a technical training. But by wanting to anticipate the needs of the economy on too long term a basis, one risks making enormous mistakes . . . (since techniques are developing so fast). In fact, behind this position of the business man, there are a number of presuppositions. There is most probably a political distruct toward the school and the university. Auxiliaries providing only a purely technical training are likely to ask less questions.

On the other hand, the Investigating Committee on the State and Development of Public Education in Italy, formed by virtue of the law of July 24, 1962, states in the conclusions of its report dealing with universities and scientific research:

. . . It is unimaginable that a quantitative adaptation of university structures alone can bring about a satisfying solution to the present problems of their development. For example, according to the latest evaluations, the ensemble of persons occupying leading posts constituted, in 1961, 3.2 percent of all Italian productive forces. In a modern structure, it seems normal that the category of leaders surpass 6 percent and that, among those, the majority have a university training. It is certainly not possible to attain this level in a period of ten to fifteen years. Already the request formulated by some to triple the annual output of graduates by 1975 thrusts a heavy task upon the university.

On the other hand, many significant facts prove that the present production of the university is much too low compared to what it should be. For example, in spite of the fact that the number of teachers and assistants increased in a non-negligible manner between 1951 and 1960, the annual number of graduates remained at a constant figure of about 20,000 units; this figure constitutes about 50 percent of admissions during the same period. The conclusions which can be drawn from these elements must be examined with great care. Nevertheless, a conscientious analysis, taking all the facts into account, shows that the ratio between the number of graduates and those admitted is much too low and that the average duration of studies is notably higher than the customary duration of studies.

This clearly indicates that it is necessary to proceed as rapidly as possible to a serious reform, in order to increase considerably the efficiency of studies; without such a reform, the increase of admissions which will manifest itself in the coming years will end up by reducing further the efficiency of education, with totally negative results.

The reform of structure must take into account that present university training is not organized to reply in an efficient and differentiated manner to the various requirements to which satisfaction must be given. If we refer here as an example to the technical faculty, we see that, if it seems opportune to be able to have on hand in 1975 a number of engineers three or four times more than the present number, the real requirements of the world of production show clearly, however, that two-thirds or three-fourths of these engineers must have a training of a much more practical and applied nature than that given today, more oriented towards the solution of purely technological problems. We do not see the necessity of giving to this category of engineers a scientific preparation as profound as the one bestowed today on all, a preparation which, on the contrary, must be reserved to that reduced fraction called upon to confront the problems of calculation and projection; while another fraction, even more reduced, must be trained with special care to attend to the needs of education and research. Needs of this nature are to be found more or less in all professions. It appears then essential to differentiate university training in general in terms of an orientation either towards purely professional aims, or professional aims fundamentally scientific, or else, purely scientific aims.

We think that such a solution will permit not only an increase in the efficiency of university studies, but also the solution of another problem which, in the coming years, will rise up in an acute form. It is clear, indeed, that the problem of the development of the university cannot be considered apart, nor as an exclusive function of the leading class; it is closely connected with secondary education. Now, the fact which must be taken into account here is that more than 60 percent of those who finish their secondary studies get admitted into the university, thus leaving insufficient enrollment for intermediary professional training. It is certain that a better articulation of higher studies could facilitate in a decisive way the solution of this problem of intermediary professionals.

If these recommendations were to be put into practice, they would certainly not fail to provoke a reaction on the part of Italian student and professorial leadership. The president of the General Federation of Arts' students (Federation generale des etudiants en Lettres, Sorbonne), Jacques Serment, commenting on Minister Fouchet's reforms of the Faculty of Arts, said:

The question is not one of learning, but of learning how to learn, and that the university does not seem disposed to understand. The student takes notes, learns, and writes. When Fouchet takes interest in the university, he is referring to an abstract university, a university without heart or soul, without students and professors. He is concerned only with the students' failure in the examinations. Nothing more . . . One is indignant, one starts hunting the 'lazy bums' while the social and material conditions of the student and pedagogical monstrosities account for this immense fiasco. But our technocrats, impregnated by rationality, on the constant look out for the least price, are not interested. Which, once more, should not surprise us; all these problems demand solutions which they do not want nor can impose. As for us, we have made our choice.[14]

What is this choice? To get the student out of the "university ghetto" which imposes a redefinition of the content of higher education in which the new sciences must be fully integrated, after which education must be adapted to the increasing complexities of production techniques. Serment continues:

It is in an enlarged conception of training that the old demand for culture, the broadening of the mind, can take its full sense today." Then only can the dilemma between a general education, product of the traditional university humanism, and a specialized education, exigency of a modern society in full mutation, be solved. Conjointly, a redefinition of teaching methods is necessary, a progressive and methodical acquisition brought about by the so-called necessity for rapid training of intermediary professionals (cadres moyens) and teachers.

And above all, training must be sufficiently general so as to permit the student not to become the slave of the techniques he will be using, to enable him to assess his knowledge in comparison with other subjects of learning, and to have a critical view of the structures and the social relations in which he will be living. With respect to democratization, students advocate, after an "unrivaled" secondary education, a common orientation cycle for all students to reveal the aptitudes of each individual.

This new current of democratization and assessment of educational assumptions among the students (a majority in France, Belgium, and Italy) finds its supporters among the academics, who, in March 1966, joined with the students in a strike at the Sorbonne in opposition to the reforms disclosed in France on February 24, 1966, and among the labor unions striving to reinforce their links with the university community: particularly so in France, where labor unionists participated in the conference on The Langevin-Wallon Plan of Reform of Education, organized by the French Group of New Education and the French Society of Pedagogy in 1964. This participation stems from a general movement toward unification of all "democratic forces," subsequent to the new role that the academic community sees for itself in the general cultural and social development of each individual.

As we pointed out above, the general principle prevailing with respect to higher education is that it should not only prepare the individual for a research or teaching career, but also to occupy other functions in society; that it should satisfy the economy's needs and that it should be democratic. The government and business answer for France is the creation of the "Institut Universitaire de Technologie"; and for the Netherlands, the "Baccalaureaat" B.A., a two-year training period which will train professionals for those new intermediatory functions closely associated with the work of engineers, researchers, and high administrative, financial, and business professionals.

The Dutch student reaction:

The instauration of the "baccalaureaat" will bring about a rationalization of higher education in two ways: (1) it implies the conscious preparation to practical life through an appropriate program of studies, and (2) whereas today the only final route in higher education in the Netherlands is towards the "Doctoraat," it will provide a goal for those who prefer shorter studies; consequently the "doctoraat" classes will be less crowded. Furthermore, higher education will then have a pluralistic object (science and teaching on the one hand, professional training on the other). These two elements need not be antagonistic, but complementary, and they could be described as the "know-how" and "know-why."[15]

And the Dutch student organization adds: "The baccalaureaat is a form of democratization ... the studies are shorter and thus, psychologically, more adapted to students coming from the working class."

With this new dimension added to higher education, it is agreed upon by government, industry, and business, and even by Dutch students, that democratization, quality, and society's needs are safe.

Is that really so? It seems to many that at least two basic factors of education are denied: orientation, i.e., democratization, and quality.

It is admitted by almost everyone that social inequality, and subsequent cultural inequality, determine the aptitude of children and adolescents to assimilate the culture bestowed upon them in the schools and the universities. Thus, the students are, as they are called in a recent published book, "inheritants," inheritants of a culture which is that of the social milieu to which they belong. And by creating theoretical sections and practical sections one favors this "natural segregation." "The children coming from the popular classes, discriminated against at the start, will find themselves in the train of the failed ones ... On the other hand, the more well-to-do will see their children crowned with laurels and become 'brilliant subjects'."[16]

If previously one denounced the obsolete structures of the university, not adapted to the aspirations of many students, now one denounces the pre-university "orientation" operating at the close of secondary studies. This orientation, many say, will be done in terms of the social, thus cultural, background of the student because university structures have not been changed. And the student coming from the working-class will more easily direct himself toward the Institut Universitaire de Technologie, where the promise of a professional training is tempting but delusive. "True democratization can only be achieved by a common education for all children from the first grade on."

As for quality, students and professors alike, in France, doubt whether it will be possible to train a highly qualified technician within a two-year period. If it seems possible for electronics, it does not seem so for mechanics. However it is, the French Higher Council for National Education (Conseil supérieur de l'Education national), disposing of a consultative voice in the Ministry of Education and composed of representatives of all cycles of study (private and public), and the Union of Technical Education (Syndicat de l'Enseignement technique) have opposed the creation of these institutes. It is, furthermore, understood that many faculties of science will attempt to make mere appendixes of the institutes which threaten their monopoly. This experience (by 1972, according to the Fifth Plan, 125,000 students will attend the IUT) can be successful only if they distinguish themselves profoundly, in their pedagogy and curriculum, from the university. Minister Fouchet's plan also allows students who failed at the final examination of the first cycle at the university (two years) to enroll at the IUT and acquire the degree of "higher technician" after one year of study only, which naturally risks making of the IUT a "second-class" institution.

The French student leaders are aware of the danger of the IUT's educational assumptions:

These measures are justified by the lack of 'technicians,' a vaguely defined term used to put across the concept of a restricted education, deprived of sufficient theoretical bases. This kind of education makes the technician a modern slave deprived of any liberty because he is refused a sufficient theoretical training . . . which would enable him to pursue his studies later and adapt himself constantly to the demands and developments of his trade.

Referring to planning in education, Mr. Fourastie points out the difficulties in forecasting: "It is not only difficult to forecast the number of engineers we will need in 1975 and of what level . . . but what those engineers will have to know in 1975."[17]

The drama then is that one has to train people who will live in a world we do not know and about which we have only some vague insights. "I could not insist enough on this: we have to form our children much more to an intellectual elasticity than to the knowledge of certain techniques known today. We must give them, above all, the aptitude to form themselves to the techniques that they will have to apply in 1975."[18]

The preoccupations then of governments, business, and industry in Europe seem, if we take into consideration the conclusions of the Italian commission, the remarks of Maurice Duverger, the recommendations of the Dutch Commission of Education (1949) concerning the creation of the "baccalaureaat," and the deliberations of the Ministers of Education of the different Lander in Germany, who are considering a shortening of studies, to be guided by the immediate needs of the economy and the civil service (by the reforms in France a secondary school teacher will be trained in three years instead of four) − at the expense of democratization, quality, and respect for individual freedom.

On the other hand, the university is concerned with its quality and the training of researchers, ("the only way to maintain Europe independent,") which now, so one likes to believe, is threatened, due to the greater number of students; whence stems the increasing interest in a selective entrance system into the university.

2 Democratization

The university has undergone profound changes these last years, first because there are many more students, secondly because there are many more students, and finally, because there are many more students [Christian Fouchet, French Minister of Education to the National Committee of UNEF, February 1966].

It is not good to live in a country where there exists an excess of highly qualified persons, because in a period of crisis, youths who have studied for a long time and find themselves without a suitable position present not only a clearcut loss considering the investments which had to be made, but even more so a risk to the established order [President, General-Manager, Kodak-Pathe, S.A.].

Preparation for University and Democratization

As we reviewed the factors which brought about the considerable expansion of higher education in Europe, it became clear that expansion, to the extent that it touched social classes previously weakly represented in the university, resulted in some sort of democratization. We might qualify this as "economic" demo-cratization — or "popularization," with all the restrictions that this term implies — dealing, as we have seen, a serious blow to the traditional university, its educational assumptions and structures, and increasing its already serious material problems. Expansion-democratization-popularization became then the key to discussions at all levels in Europe, in every domain — pedagogical, political, economic, financial, and planificational.

But before taking into consideration democratization at the university level, and because of the organization of the European educational systems and their continuity from the primary school up to the highest levels of education, we must first present the situation at the secondary school level, which, as we already pointed out, remains "par excellence" the preparatory stage to higher education. Most observers in Europe have stated that if a true expansion and democratization of education is to be brought about, it is at the secondary school level that European authorities should intervene. In his recently published book, Poignant, pointing out in his main conclusion that European education suffers from a considerable lag in the output of graduates, states that the problem of the school systems lies at the secondary level.[1]

If we have to extensively take into consideration the secondary school systems in Europe it is because, contrary to the United States, where, among other differences, compulsory courses in Greek and Latin at the secondary school level are absent and where "parallel" educational systems never existed, secondary education in Europe conditions university education from every point of view (economic, political, pedagogical, financial, etc.), and because it appears more clearly every day that democratization as much as regional disparities are taken increasingly into considerstion by planning boards.

According to an organization which goes back to the 19th century, primary school in Europe finishes at the age of ten or twelve, varying from country to country. Then, a choice has to be made in "terms of the child's aptitudes and the desires of the parents." Indeed, two routes can be followed. The first simply continues education within the primary school structure for which primary school teachers are qualified. It is generally known as the "higher cyclus of primary education" coming to an end with the school age limit, that is, at fourteen or fifteen years of age. The second leads to entrance into the secondary school. In Belgium and the Netherlands, children can also enter professional training schools or technical schools upon completion of the primary school. We will consider here only the secondary school.

If we cannot, in the frame of this study, present all the details of the secondary school system, we will nevertheless outline those characteristics which seem to us most illustrative of the pedagogical conception of the secondary school and the advancement of "democratization" in the various countries.

In the 19th century, classical studies (Greek and Latin) had to be paid for and were thus open only to children coming from the well-to-do classes without any particular intellectual selection. They determined not only the role of the secondary school — preparation for the university — but also gave it the social prestige which permitted it to remain the model. Later, new sections (modern studies, sciences) and new schools developed. For Britain, A. K. C. Ottaway notes in *Education of Society — Introduction to the Sociology of Education*:

The secondary schools would imitate the public schools with their academic, classical, and linguistic functions; with their games, their monitors, their colors, and their old school ties; a whole repertory of social distinctions and of aristocratic mentality. Thousands of students crowded into the secondary schools seeking the possibility of becoming wealthier, of reaching a loftier social position. The prevalent aims were always the same and the pedagogical principles accepted by the members of the new professions and of the suburban white collar groups were those of the upper classes. What did it matter whether the teaching did or did not correspond to the actual requirements of their future careers? As long as attending the secondary schools means getting better jobs, the parents are willing to let their children learn anything, provided that they pass their exams and earn their diplomas.[2]

Even more clearly, the Spens report of 1938 asserts: "The tradition was so strong that when the state, on the basis of the education act of 1902, undertook for the first time the overall organization of the secondary schools, the old classical school, local or not local, became the almost exclusive model for the secondary school."[3]

And if one remembers that the "lycee" of the 19th century was shaped according to the "mother" school of the Jesuits ratio studiorum, holding on to the same general spirit and methods of education set forth at the Renaissance, one can imagine how limited the changes were. Even in the new sections of the secondary school, differences with the classical studies come out only in the curricula:

But they are minor. Greek may be taken out and more physics and mathematics added; or, both Greek and Latin may be removed and business techniques, accounting, technology, quantitative chemical analysis and chemical plant design may be added. But the basic pattern remains the same, all the more so if one considers that very often the teachers of the technical subjects themselves had gotten to the university by way of the (classical) lyceum.[4]

But later that century, under social and economic pressure, the secondary "short" schools developed, recruiting their students among the children of the "petite bourgeoisie" (artisans, small businessman, white collar labor) wanting training to become medium professionals. As for the mass of children, they barely completed the primary mandatory education, which had become mandatory very late, around the turn of the century, and in Belgium in 1914. Then, at the close of the First World War, under the pressure of what we could call the first "vague democratique," these situations of discriminatory school policy were denounced in most of the European countries. The principle of democratization being then progressively adopted, the authorities moved towards the "democratization" of the secondary schools of which the results today are: (1) the existence, along with classical studies, of modern studies; and (2) secondary schools are free of cost, and scholarships are granted to needy students.

Leaving temporarily aside the recent reforms which we will discuss later, the secondary school system in the Common Market countries can be divided into two sections: (1) secondary long education; (2) secondary short education.

Secondary long education. This type of education, demanding from six to nine years beyond the time required for completion of primary education, prepares its students directly for higher education. Its traditional task is to give them the necessary basic culture, scientific as well as literary, to enable them to undertake higher education with the greatest benefit. It is only in recent years that jobs are offered to graduates of the secondary school filling the functions of medium professionals and receiving, in most cases, a professional training in the institution for which they work. But upon entrance into the "lycee" the child has another choice to make, decisive in most cases: which section should be chosen? There are usually five: classical studies (Greek and Latin); Latin and science: Latin and modern languages; modern section concentrating on science, or modern section concentrating on economics and social sciences. One can reasonably claim that the section chosen does preorient the university studies, and may, indeed, definitively determine the type of higher education, since the "polyvalence" of the secondary school is not granted in every country. There also exists, in fact, and for the reasons we have previously outlined, what has been called an "hierarchy of cultures" with, at the summit, Greek and Latin towards which children from the higher social classes are oriented; then the modern section with its "economic" subdivision mainly composed of children of the low middle class and, in some cases, working class. Next comes the "secondary short education," after which remains the technical institutes and the professional schools. Certainly, as we shall see, the differences are less pronounced today as there is no longer such a "classe depotoire." But the fact remains that to many there is one "royal route" in secondary education – the Greek and Latin section.

Secondary short education. If in all European countries the final goal of secondary long education is entrance into the university, secondary short education's final goal differs from country to country, but it does exist in every European country. The period of study varies from three to five years beyond the time required for completion of primary school.

In Belgium, the studies in the "ecoles moyennes" (medium schools) correspond exactly to the first cycle of the secondary long education (three years). Children, at the age of 15, can normally continue their studies in the second cycle of the secondary long education, as indeed 60 percent of them do. In France, the program of study of the "college d'enseignement general" CEG (College of General Education) corresponds to the first cycle of the modern section of the "lycees." The students of the CEG, having successfully passed their examinations, can enter the modern sections, second cycle, of the lycee, or the technical sections. About 50 percent of the graduates of the CEG choose this possibility.

In France and Belgium, then, secondary short education is only a variation of secondary long education for which it prepares its students adequately. But the distinctions between the various sections are maintained.

In Germany, however, for graduates of the Realschülen, (secondary short education), entrance to the final classes of the Gymnasium is quite exceptional because of the differences in the programs of study between the two types of secondary schools. But several Länder have developed a special entrance examination allowing Realschülen graduates to enter special sections of secondary long education (Gymnasiale Aufbauklassen).

In Italy, graduates of the "avviamento professionnale" can enter only the professional schools (training of workers and employees) and, upon entrance examination, the technical institutes. As for the Netherlands, graduates of secondary short education can, as in Italy, enter only the technical schools and the teacher training schools for primary school teachers.

Most of these democratization policy measures were carried out during the period between the two world wars, and were in use until 1959-1964, depending on the country. After more than forty years of effort toward democratization, the results have not been very satisfactory, as Tables 2-1 and 2-2 show.

To be sure, the above tables show that over a period of ten years the variation in the development of the number of students attending secondary school in terms of their social origin is considerable for the working classes, but progress for these classes is so much more easily noticed as the starting point was so much lower.

According to German sources, the percentage of a given age group attending secondary long education over the next ten years will remain at 8 percent. This would mean a regression for the lower social classes, as it is indeed most unlikely that higher social classes will change their customs and cease to send their

Table 2-1

The Netherlands:[a] Evolution in the
Rate of Schoolgoing at the Age of 12
in Secondary Long Education, in
Terms of the Social Origin

Social categories	Males				Females			
	1942	*1949*	*1960*	*Variation 1942-1960*	*1942*	*1949*	*1960*	*Variation 1942-1960*
Higher	45	50	67	+ 35%	36	45	63	+ 40%
Medium	14	15	25	+ 66%	7	9	10	+ 43%
Working class	4	4	7	+ 75%	2	2	4	+100%
Average	10	11	17	+ 54%	6	7	13	+ 85%

[a]Source: Document DAS-EIP — 62-22
de l'OCDE.

children to the Gymnasium. Will the same phenomenon also appear in other countries? It seems that the same could be said for the Netherlands, as is pointed out by Raymond Poignant. It may be noted that it is precisely in those two countries where the possibility of switching from one section to another, or the "polyvalence" of the secondary school degrees, is not granted.

But whatever the increase is in the number of children attending secondary school, considerable differences remain in terms of social origin. The causes of these differences are well known. The two most often cited are: the standard of living which increasingly becomes a lesser factor determining attendance of secondary long education because of the general increase in the standard of living, even for the lowest social classes, and the social aid given to needy and worthy students; and the traditional cultural advantages of the socially elite classes who traditionally choose secondary long education, preferably the classical section. This cultural tradition, without doubt, also brings with it a professional tradition (liberal professions, leading posts in industry, business, administration, and university). For the middle and lower social classes, the same cultural traditions do not exsit and the professional aspirations of their children are more modest, because as we shall see, the lower social income groups feel that seven years of secondary education not leading ultimately to any professional qualification look hazardous. They prefer to choose a more practical training which they can find in the technical schools of the secondary level.

But a third less often cited factor, which is a limitative one for the children coming from the lower social classes, is the type of education offered. With this

Table 2-2

France: Evolution in the Rate of Admission in the First Year of the
Secondary School Between 1954 and
1962, in Terms of Social Origin

Profession of Parents	1954[a] total %	1962[b] total %	Variations
Higher professionals	84	94	+ 11
Liberal professions	87	93	+ 7
Industrialists and big businessmen	68	85	+ 26
Medium professionals	47	84	+ 78
Employees	43	67	+ 55
Artisans and small businessmen	39	66	+ 69
Industry workers	21	45	+114
Farmers	16	40	+150
Agricultural workers	13	32	+146
Medium	29	55	+ 89

[a]The whole of France less the department of   [b]The whole of France.
the Seine (Paris) which reduces the percent-
age for the higher prof. and liberal prof. in
1954.

factor we touch a limiting element inherent in the structure and the concepts of
the role of the secondary school in the society, and hence, in the university. The
problem of which type of study is most suitable for children coming from lower
social classes, so as to enable them to reach the highest levels of education, is not
on the verge of solution. This would require a pedagogical revolution which is
not likely to take place within the next few years and which depends largely on
the type of education and training future teachers of the secondary school
receive at the university.

Attitude of the teachers. Earlier we pointed out that students today are attending a university whose goals no longer correspond to the goals that the students have set forth themselves, and that consequently the type of education offered appears to many irrelevent or outdated. If the same cannot be said with an equal emphasis for the secondary schools, nevertheless it is true that if one considers the type of program offered today, one notices the great similarity to the type of program offered in the Jesuits' colleges of the 18th century, where Latin was the central object of study. But with the devaluation of Latin in later years, and with the increasing independence of the teacher from the school director's 18th century dictatorship, each teacher came to consider "his" subject as the center of learning around which other subjects circle. "From the autonomy of the teachers was born their rivalry, and this rivalry in its turn gave birth to what has been called 'rivalry of the disciplines'."[5] Reforms in the programs are not considered simply as reforms by the teachers, but as victories or defeats for their subjects. Furthermore, each teacher holds on to the monopoly of his subject to which he adds the new branches discovered or developed over a number of years. The most often cited example is geography, to which was added paleontology, geology, and economics. This in itself is a good procedure as the teacher can then in his particular subject give a synthesis of knowledge to his students. But, on the other hand, at the university level, specialization is so extreme that there are different types of highly esteemed degrees (aggregation for example in France), the object of which is to train researchers. This phenomenon then poses the more general problem that confronts universities all over the world. How, indeed, can they respond to their traditional double object: train teachers for the secondary schools and train researchers? In former times these two tasks of the university were complementary, inseparable. But today, with the development of science, the subdivision into various specialities demands a long preparation in one particular field which fails to give the general culture that secondary school teachers must possess.

Conscious of these problems, educators, academic authorities, governments, ministries of education, parents and student association in Europe are at present attempting to solve them. In France, for example, the reforms which will be introduced have taken this problem into account and provide a different type of training for teachers and researchers. That is, students entering the Faculty of Sciences and the Faculty of Letters and Human Sciences will follow the same courses for two years. At the end of this two-year term, and according to the advice given them by their professors, they can choose either to finish their higher education in one year to become a teacher (licence) or in two years to enter research, in principle at least (maitrise, newly created degree).

If the principle of this reform is excellent in itself, its application provokes lively reactions on the part of the teachers, especially those who will have to teach in the lower cycle of the secondary school and for whom no specific reform is foreseen and who are surely expressing their fear of seeing their posts taken over by the "licenciés." Furthermore, will the "maitrise" — a different degree with a different final object and possibly more highly esteemed because of the greater difficulty of obtaining it — differentiate too much the students and professionals later?

Some scholars believe that a unique opportunity for the change in the spirit, methods, programs, and structures of education has been missed on two occasions. Vermot-Gauchy points out that everything was possible between 1866 and 1901 when various laws brought about the creation and organization of the primary school, the primary superior schools, and the secondary schools for girls. During that period the number of teachers tripled and one could have trained the teachers as one wished. After this date it was too late since, for the first half of this century, the number of teachers increased with an annual average of only 0.5 percent. The second occasion was missed, according to Vermot-Gauchy, in 1950 when the forecasting of needs was sufficiently precise and since, from 1950 to 1970, the number of teachers was to be increased two to three times (from 192,000 to 447,000). If measures had been taken at that time, the result would be that teachers recruited these last fifteeen years would not have been trained according to the old methods and the old programs.[6]

As we will see later in this chapter, in reference to the reforms introduced at the secondary school level in various European countries, the problem of the teachers, their training and attitudes toward these reforms, and their role within them, is considerable and has been one of the main concerns of the reformers.

The organization of the secondary school system explains, for quite similar reasons, the relatively small percentage of students coming from lower social classes who attend the university.

After more than thirty years of efforts toward democratization — many of the measures described with relation to the secondary school system date from the period between the two world wars — the percentage of students coming from the lower social classes remains very low (see Tables 2-3, 2-4, 2-5, 2-6, and 2-7), while these same classes (factory workers, agricultural workers) still represent the bulk of the active population; in France, for example, 56 percent.

Undoubtedly, one can still speak of a "class," if not "caste," aspect of secondary and consequently higher education in Europe, although at the close of the Second World War, these differences were denounced in the European countries. The best example is the Langevin-Wallon commission in France which has been, and still is, the main reference for the democratic forces in France. Outside of France, the Langevin-Wallon principles and programs have also retained considerable attention in all social circles.

The Langegin — Wallon committee laid down four principles:

1. The first principle, which dominates all the others, is justice. "It presents two aspects, not in the least opposed to one another, but complementary: equality and diversity. All children, whatever their family, social, or ethnic background is, have an equal right to the maximum development of their personality. They should not find any other limitation than their own aptitude. Education must thus offer to all equal possibilities of development, open to all the access to culture."

2. "Equality necessitates the recognition of the equal dignity of all the social tasks, of the high material and moral value of manual activities, of practical intelligence, of technical value."

Table 2-3

**Belgium:[a] Distribution of the Number
of Students at the University of
Louvain, in Terms of the Social Origin
(1959-60)**

| | Students Admittted | | Approximate |
Profession of Parents	Dutch Roll %	French Roll %	Average %
1. Agriculturalists	6.8	4.5	5.74
2. Chiefs of industry and commerce	26.6	22.0	24.40
a. Chiefs of enterprise	7.0	11.2	9.00
b. Artisans & small traders	19.6	10.8	15.40
3. Liberal professions and upper staff	24.2	43.3	33.31
a. Liberal professions & professions requiring a university degree	15.4	26.1	20.48
b., c. High ranking civil servants — magistrates	6.9	14.7	10.59
d. Professors	1.9	2.5	2.24
e. Superior staff private	included in 3a.		
4. Average staff	20.8	18.7	19.77
a. Civil service	4.5	5.8	5.13
b. Teachers	7.5	2.9	5.27
c. Private sector	8.8	10.0	9.37
5. Clerks	10.4	5.6	8.20
6. Industrial laborers & inferior staff	8.4	3.0	5.77
7. Other categories or unknown profession	2.8	2.8	2.81

[a]Inquest of the service of the "Universitaire
Werkgemeenschap" of Louvain, 1959-60.

Table 2-4

Belgium:[a] University of Brussels—Comparative Structures of the Belgian Students Enrolling for the First Time, from 1962-63 to 1964-65, in Terms of Father's Profession

Categories	62/63	%	63/64	%	64/65	%	Av. for 3 yrs.
1. Farmers (owners)	10	1.0	7	0.5	12	0.8	0.8
2. Retailers	88	8.5	118	8.6	146	9.4	8.8
3. Industrialists	106	10.2	88	6.5	89	5.7	7.5
4. Liberal professions	68	6.6	112	8.2	110	7.1	7.3
5. Independent	52	5.0	74	5.4	68	4.4	4.9
6. Workers (labor)	94	9.1	96	7.0	137	8.8	8.3
7. Subaltern agents	56	5.4	87	6.4	117	7.5	6.4
8. Medium professionals	179	17.3	252	18.5	285	18.3	18.0
9. Teachers	64	6.1	70	5.1	91	5.8	5.7
10. Higher professionals	176	17.0	244	17.9	306	19.6	18.2
11. University prof., magistrates	21	2.0	24	1.8	21	1.3	1.7
12. No profession, retired	35	3.4	40	2.9	52	3.3	3.2
13. Dead or absent	76	7.3	136	10.0	124	8.0	8.4
14. Various (prof. undetermined, etc.)	11	1.1	13	0.9	1	-	0.7
15. Without reply	-	-	4	0.3	-	-	0.9
Total	1,036	100	1,365	100	1,559	100	100

[a]Source: Institut de Socilogie de l'Universite Libre de Bruxelles, "Evolution structurelle et democratisat on des etudes a l'Universite Libre de Bruxelles," Brussels, 1965, Charles D'Hoogh - 23, Chart 18.

Table 2-5

The Netherlands:[a] Distribution of the
Number of Students of Higher Education, in Terms of Social Origin

Profession of Parents	1947-48 %	1958-59 %
Agriculturists (cultivating owners)	4.3	5.0
Company directors	8.6	8.9
Artisans and businessmen	17.8	15.1
Civil servants:		
a) Staff	23.9	23.8
b) Executive staff	11.9	9.0
Liberal professions	12.1	13.4
Business and industry employees		
a) Staff	6.9	6.4
b) Others	11.3	11.4
Industry and agricul. workers	1.0	5.2
No or unknown profession	2.2	1.8
General Total	100	100

[a]Source: Raymond Poignant, "L'enseignement dans les pays du Marche Commun,"
Paris, 1966, Chart No. 75, p. 203.

3. "The exploitation of natural aptitudes ... determining the principle of
orientation. First educational orientation, then professional orientation must
lead to placing each worker, each citizen in the post for which his possibilities
are the best adapted, the one most favorable to his output."
4. Since general culture represents what unites men, while the profession
represents too often what separates them, "a solid general culture must serve as
the basis for professional specialization and must be pursued during the training

Table 2-6

Federal Republic of Germany:[a] **Distribution of the Number of Students at the University, in Terms of Social Origin**

	In percentage of total	
Parent's Profession	males	females
Agriculturists (cultivating)	3.6	3.0
Businessmen and Industrialists	14.6	13.8
Liberal professions	11.3	15.5
Civil servants	32.8	36.5
Clerks[b]	30.0	27.0
Workers	6.0	2.8
No profession	1.7	1.3

[a]Source: Raymond Poignant, "L'enseignement dans les pays du Marche Commun," Paris, 1966, Chart No. 73, p. 201.

[b]This heading includes probably medium and higher professionals of the private sector.

so that the training of the man will not be limited and hindered by the training of the technician."

An ideal, surely, and our task here is not to comment on ideals, but to try to present as well as possible, not so much the intensity with which this ideal is accepted, but the ways and means by which various groups in the countries considered intend to implement and approach the ideal; and therefore we stated in the beginning of this study that democratization of education contains the elements for a social, political, and economic revolution, not to speak of the pedagogical.

It appears that there are at least two distinct pedagogical conceptions which we will call: (1) democratization of the *institution,* i.e., that all the schools, secondary as well as higher, be considered as of equally important educational value and cultural prestige no matter for what further profession they prepare, which seems to us to correspond to the second principle of the Langevin-Wallon commission; and (2) democratization of the *teaching* within the existing institutions. We mean by that the postponement to a more advanced age of the choice that children have to make of the type of study they will follow upon

Table 2-7

**France: Distribution of the Number of
Students in the Public Faculties, in
Terms of Social Origin** (1961-62)

Profession of Parents	% in the active population census 1962	% on the whole of the faculties[a]	Number of students per 1,000 active persons
1. Agriculturists	15.7	5.6	3.0
2. Farm hands	4.3	0.6	1.4
3. Chiefs of industry & commerce	10.4	17.7	- - -
Traders	0.4	4.0	107
Merchants	6.6	9.8	16
Artisans	3.3	3.9	13
4. Liberal professions and higher professional	4.0	28.5	- - -
Liberal profession	0.7	9.9	168
Professors[b]	0.7	5.8	91
Higher professional[b]	2.6	13.2	55
5. Average professional:	7.8	17.8	- - -
Teachers[b]	2.2	5.8	39
Average professional[b]	5.6	12.0	24
6. Clerks	12.6	7.9	7
7. Laborers:	36.7	6.4	- - -
Foreman	1.6	1.6	11 .
Laborers	27.8	4.2	1.4
Unskilled laborer	7.3	0.6	0.8
8. Personnes de Service	5.4	0.9	1.8
9. Others[c]	3.1	14.6	11

[a]Source: Information statistiques No. 53-54.   [c]Including rentiers, army, clergy and police.

[b]Public and Private.

completion of primary school, since premature choice and selection favor students coming from the higher social classes. To bring this about one organizes a "common" secondary education up to the end of the first cycle (twelve to fifteen years of age, or three years of secondary education) or, a second route, one leaves open the possibility of switching from one type of secondary education to the other. The first measure receives the approval of those favorable to greater social justice. They believe that a common secondary short education will significantly, if not completely, diminish the influence of the social and family milieu in which the children have lived and that later on the child will be oriented toward higher studies or professional training. This measure of "tronc commun" also corresponds to the principles laid down by the Langevin-Wallon commission and, as a matter of fact, was specifically asked for by the commission.

Democratization of the institutions. There is a need to adapt the educational system to the characteristics of children coming from various social backgrounds and, more precisely, to those coming from modest social classes, who, if their milieu does not permit them to develop all their faculties and interests at an early age, do develop different but equally important aptitudes and acquire another experience of life which gives them a different outlook on life where the practical is considered more important:

Because of their family origin, the nature of their spirit, the goals they set for themselves, our students of the technical schools are, more than others, close to the concrete and the real. While young they participate in the financial worries of their families and the difficulties of the economic condition. They await with impatience their entrance into the world of work. Like all adolescents they cannot express what divides them and what tears them. Because they are more engaged in life than their comrades of the secondary schools, and because they know where they want to arrive without knowing whether they will succeed, they might also have more difficulty in identifying themselves and expressing themselves. When they will be able to do so, they will not be young anymore.[7]

It is believed then that the technical schools offer the best possibilities for democratization of higher education. In 1954 in France 20 percent of the engineers and about 100,000 highly qualified techicians, artisans, and even company directors, had received their first training in the professional secondary schools.[8]

Along this line the following statistics for France (Table 2-8) show that parents of the lower social classes will more easily send their children to a professional or technical school than to the lycee — and this for seven years of study — since there will never really be any question of the child's professional future, and a different kind of language, "the abstract and 'cultured' language" is used. It might also be that parents want their children, if conditions make it necessary, to be able to stop going to school and to immediately get a good job for which their technical school has already prepared them.

Table 2-8

France:[a] Distribution of the Number of
Students in the Public Institutions of
the Second Degree of General, Professional, and Technical Education, in
Terms of Social Origin (1961-62)

Profession of Parents	% of the active population	Type of Institution			
		I.C.M. (1) %	I.T. (2) %	C.E.G. (3) %	C.E.T. (4) %
Farmers	15.7	6.5	6.0	10.0	6.0
Agricultural workers	4.3	1.2	1.7	2.7	3.9
Industry and business managers	10.4	- - -	- - -	- - -	- - -
Industrialists	(0.4)	2.1	1.7	0.8	0.5
Businessmen	(6.6)	9.2	7.4	7.4	3.8
Artisans	(3.0)	5.3	6.1	6.3	4.6
Liberal professions and higher professionals	4.0	17.1	5.7	2.4	1.4
Medium professionals	7.8	15.9	11.1	10.6	5.6
Employees	12.6	17.0	17.4	16.7	11.9
Workers	36.7	15.9	32.5	35.0	49.9
House personnel (servants)	5.4	1.2	2.0	1.8	3.1
Retired − Without profession	3.1	2.5	3.4	1.8	3.9
Other categories	- - -	6.1	5.0	4.5	5.4
Total	100	100	100	100	100

(1) Classifical and modern Lycee; (2) Technical Lycee; (3) Colleges de'enseignement general
(4) Colleges d'enseignement techniques

[a]Source: "Informations statistiques," Ministry of National Education, numbers 49-50,
June, 1963.

Moreover, the traditional secondary school is the least of all disposed to democratize, given its long tradition, its concentration on culture, and a program of teaching that does not really immediately prepare for any profession but for higher studies. As a matter of fact, studies throughout Europe have shown that dropouts are considerable in the course of studies at the secondary traditional school (see Table 2-9), which probably stems, as for the university, from the fact that the classical secondary school and the university adapted themselves over a number of years to the characteristics of children coming from the higher social classes.

Democratization of the studies. The reforms and experiments studied in the European countries considered, and presently underway, can be divided into two categories. The first is characterised by a common period of study for all children up to the first year of the second cycle of secondary school (generally at age twelve to fifteen). The second maintains the parallel structures which we presented earlier, but offers the possibility of switching from one section to another in the course of study.

The two principal preoccupations of these reforms and experiments are social justice and pedagogy. The whole system which has been functioning for so many years, deciding the future of the child at the age of ten to twelve, is denounced as undemocratic. To have working class children choosing modern or technical sections with limited possibilities in regard to higher education, and children coming from the high social classes choosing or oriented toward the most promising classical sections is absurd, since it is not conceivable that one can detect in the child at that age his real aptitudes, whether it be to discourage him from pursuing studies or, on the contrary, to encourage him. One also hopes that through these reforms it will be possible to save an intelligence which would otherwise have been lost.

The reforms and studies have been carried out in the various European countries, in very different ways. These differences stem mainly, as we shall see, from the financial investment that these reforms presuppose, but possibly much more so from the differences which exist on the level of the teachers.

The Reforms

Belgium

"L'Ecole Moyenne" — three years of study (ages twelve to fifteen) correspond in its program of study to the first three years of the secondary school (Athenee for the boys; Lycees for the girls). In the technical schools the first three years also correspond to a great extent to the first three years of the Athenee. But the system of sections (classical, modern, technical) is maintained, although, since 1959, in an experimental program authorities installed in a number of "Ecoles Moyennes," there has been cyclus of observation where all the children follow

Table 2-9

France: Evolution of a Class Entered in
the First Year (Sixth) of the Classical
and Modern Sections of the Lycee, in
Terms of the Social Origin[a]

Class	Farmers	Industry Workers	Medium Professionals	Liberal Professionals & High Professionals
Sixth class	100	100	100	100
Third class	72	59	85	92
First class	35	21	55	86[b]

[a]Source: Raymond Poignant, "L'enseignement dans les pays du Marche Commun," Paris, 1966, Chart No. 32, p. 105.

[b]These percentages are corroborated by the conclusions of a study undertaken under the direction of Professor Jean Fourastie (Conservatoire des Arts et Metiers, Laboratoire d'econometrie, Paris, 1965) on two promotions of "L'Ecole polytechnique," and "Ecole Centrale" of Paris according to which 80 percent of males and 60 percent females of these families obtained the "baccalaureat."

the same courses, are never separated from one another, and have the possibility of choosing a number of optional courses such as Latin. These measures, coupled to the ones described previously with reference to the "polyvalence" of all secondary school degrees (including technical) for entrance into the university, are expected to give the desired results both from the point of view of democratization and pedagogy.

Italy

Since the reform of 1940 (Reform Bottai) two cycles of secondary school have coexisted: "scuola media" and "scuola d'avviamento professionale." Over the last twenty years a number of other types of secondary schools have been organized (inferior cycle of "instituti d'arte," post elementary classes). In this situation one can see the double characteristics of education: classic and professional, the first corresponding to the "scuola media", the second to the "scuola d'avviamento professionale." The problem consisted in transforming and expanding these different cycles of secondary school to satisfy principles laid down in the Italian constitution and the requirements of a mass education, i.e., democratization, since the new reforms should enable children to attend school for a longer period of time and, eventually, to pursue their studies — without any barriers which existed before from the divisions into cycles — up to the university.

We will consider here at some length the Italian reform, how it came about and what its main characteristics are: first, because the Italian case is unique, setting up a "tronc commun" — a single class for all children over a period of three years; second, because the information which we have at our disposal shows the reaction of the different social and political forces with respect to this reform; and third, because the reform dealt quite remarkably with the problem of the teaching of Latin.

Mandatory education, that is, education for all up to a certain age, could only, according to some schools of thought, be organized effectively and justly in the frame of a unique school ("tronc commun") which, for the Italian communist representative Mario Alicata, "is a natural reality; the orientation of youths toward a rational comprehension of social and cultural phenomena; the conquest of humanism which, far from repudiating the values of tradition, does not mortify them by reducing them to a banal and dry study of Latin, but leaves room to the new values of science, technique, and work."

For Romano Ledda, in "l'Unita," a Communist daily, the motive which "links the access of the popular masses to learning and to the search for a new content based on the essential components of contemporary consciousness" is evident: the creation of a single school offering a humanism in which the new values of today's world would stand alongside the traditional values.

Opposed to this concept of the school as expressed by the leftist parties, the liberal parties supported the maintenance of a diversified secondary school, stating in one of their programs that "there exists in a democratic society a variety of functions; one attains some of them through studies of a certain type, and others through studies of a different type."

These differences between the various political power groups, as briefly indicated here, had for a long time stopped any move toward reorganization of the secondary school, until, in December, 1962, the political situation had improved and allowed the setting up of the single school. Its characteristics are best summarized by its promoter, Minister Gui: "Unity: interior and optional subdivisions preceded by common mandatory experiences . . . an education which gives a basic training, general and not specialized."

There remained the problem of Latin. On this issue Minister Gui, refusing to enter the quarrel between the opponents and supporters of Latin, said at the House of Representatives:

On the one hand we say 'yes' to Latin because it alone teaches how to reason, alone it is formation and humanism, alone it reacts to materialism; but on the other hand, we say 'no' to Latin, because it is another language, a dead language, because the values of modern man are different from the classical values. The new secondary school says 'yes' to humanism, to the formation brought about by the study of language and the cultural values that it holds within itself, but it assigns this role to Italian and not to Latin. That's all. To think that this role could only be assumed by Latin is a long bypassed opinion. Latin was the basis of the old 'ginnasio' because it was in former times the language of culture in opposition to the vulgar. But, for a long time now the vulgar has been for us the language of culture. . . . But still, we say 'yes' to Latin, not because it is the unreplaceable basis of all formative education, but because, in a sense, Latin is the old Italian . . . and in this sense it is no longer a language different from ours. That is why the proposed education recognises this reality by imposing it on all the schools in the second year. Those who wish later on to orient themselves toward literary studies can then in the third year pursue the study of Latin optionally.

This reform in Italy is indeed a great step forward toward democratization of secondary education, and hence of higher education, since it offers a humanistic, formative program to all children without any distinction of social background. The political forces which voted for the reform — Christian democrats, democrats, communists, and socialists — welcomed it as a real realization of justice. And an American observer, Dr. James B. Conant, a former president of Harvard University, considering the old European tradition consisting of "assigning certain particular orders of education to those who wish to attend the university," noted, in 1960, when the Italian project was being considered, that its adoption "would place Italy ahead of the other European countries with regard to reform of education."

Opponents asked for a deferment of this reform until a total reform of the educational system, including higher education had been carried out, in order not to negatively affect the higher degrees of study. This objection is indeed valid, but the realization of a total reform is time consuming, and time is pressing. At present, though, Italy is considering a complete reorganization of its higher education.

The Netherlands

The law of February 14, 1963, concerning reform of secondary education, provides that the programs of the first year of the different types of secondary school (short and long) be similar. This enables teachers and parents alike to orient the child, after this first year, to a specific type of secondary education, thus offering the possibility of horizontal switching. The same law also sees to it that priority is given to a general training before the professional training.

West Germany

For the lower cycles, efforts have been essentially limited to the possibilities of switching from one school to another through special examinations and special schools preparing for these examinations (Aufbau form). The decisions in this domain belong to the Länder.

France

The Reform of 1959 provided that children would enter an "observation cyclus" of two years organized in the "lycees" and the "college d'enseignement general." But, as Raymond Poignant points out, this orientation cycle has not been effective since it was organized in the traditional types of schools, despite the creation of "orientation committees."

A reform of 1963 extends the observation cycle to the first four years of the secondary school (first cycle) organized in the "lycees" and "college d'enseigement general." It is also provided that autonomous institutions called College d'Enseignement Secondaire (C.E.S.) will unite all the sections of the first cycle of the secondary schools. This is seen by observers as the most positive aspect of the reform. This is expected to be done over the period covered by the 5th National Plan (1966-70). As a result, with the extension of mandatory education up to a ten year period, all youth will be entering the first cyclus of secondary school and in some cases in an autonomous school of the first cyclus. But the French maintain the system of "sections" (Latin, modern, technical, etc.) and according to some, the possible inconveniences from the point of view of orientation will be diminished because of the grouping together of the different sections in the same institution.

This situation creates a lively reaction on the part of the "specialists" denouncing a "primarization" of the secondary school, a "regression" of the cultural traditions which form the basis for the "greatness" of European education. Poignant concludes that it is not so much the principle of "secondary common cyclus" which is discussed, particularly if one adopts the system of "sections," "but it is essentially the conditions of transition from the old structures to the new ones from the point of view of the teacher." We are not that optimistic. We have seen in the case of Italy, that this problem of the teachers is nonexistant, or at least considerably reduced, since the two types of secondary school systems from which one created the single secondary achool both had teachers trained at the university. Nevertheless, it has taken a long time to come to the present reform. On the other hand, we do believe, for reasons we have expressed quite often in this work, that the maintenance of sections is but a half measure still distinguishing the children too much at an early age, even when possibilities of switching from one section to another have been set up.

All these reforms have been introduced recently and effects will be seen only around 1970-75, when those entering the secondary school today under these new regulations will have graduated and entered professional life or the university. But today the question remains open: Will the secondary school be able to adapt itself through these measures to its new clients and prepare them for higher education or professional life in terms of their needs, desires, and aptitudes?

There is another question which these various reforms raise: the position of the teachers. If the reforms have been elaborated in terms of quality and democratization — and, as we shall see, in terms of the needs of the economy, the reformers also have had to deal with the subtle problem of the types of teachers and teachers' training existing in European education.

Teachers are very sensitive to this question of who will teach what and at what level. It is commonly known that the Union of Secondary School Teachers ("lycees") in France have adopted the Langevin-Wallon principle of "tronc commun" because the commission provided that the teaching should be done by specialized and university trained teachers.

To illustrate the dangers of this non-university and specialized training of teachers, one could cite the British example where the reform of 1944 (Education Act) provided for a secondary school for all children, but maintained three sections (classical, modern, technical). In spite of the efforts of the authorities to grant "parity of esteem" to the three sections, the grammar schools in fact have held the first place in the opinion of public and teachers, especially because of the quality of their teachers of which 78% are university graduates. The modern schools' percentage is only 17.[9]

The various types of prolonged education beyond the primary school, and the parallel educational systems existing in the various countries, with the exception of Italy, correspond to different types of teachers: (1) at the level of the lycees or the full secondary school teachers are university graduates (licencie); (2) at the level of secondary short education, teachers have received a short higher education (generally two years after the end of the secondary school); and (3) at the level of the higher cycle of the primary school teachers have been trained in specialized schools up to about the age of twenty.

Now if one decides to offer the same type of school – first cyclus of the secondary school in common with that in Italy, or a first cyclus with the maintenance of different sections as in France – who then are the teachers who can teach in this common secondary school cyclus? Thus, at present, there are three types of teachers at the disposal of this first cyclus, but naturally with a majority of "instituteurs" (primary school teachers). So, at least for the immediate future, the common cyclus will have to depend to a large extent on the primary school teachers, who are not "specialists" in the various subjects taught in these schools.

The problem of teacher training will not be solved very soon nor very easily and can only be considered on a long-term basis. But with the present reforms at the university level (France making the distinction between training for teachers and training for researchers), one might say that at least the possibilities for a positive outcome have been set up. All will depend on the programs, which have not yet been made public, and on the training methods which will be used. Then, for France at least, a situation of "everything is possible" will present itself again around 1975 when the teachers recruited between 1940 and 1950 will retire. This successive replacement will then be carried on up to the end of the century.

Reasons for Change and
Options for Change

For years articles, conferences, statements of unions and individuals have asserted that the reform of secondary and higher education and the crisis of the educational systems in Europe stem from ministerial instability (particularly in France and Italy), or from the pressures of academics reluctant to change, or from the business world, or from the little understanding that was received from financial departments, etc., — or even from the lack of serious studies since none of the new measures had been preceded by a "serious" analysis of the existing situation. All of these are true to a certain extent, and one might add another reason which we think has been decisive in the move toward reform and democratization that came along with it. It would be tempting to subtitle what follows "From principles to reforms, but passing by needs," since indeed, there was not until about ten years ago a real need for change — or at least, no need for change on a short-term basis. Things are quite different, however, as seen from a long-term point of view.

From the close of the Second World War up to the mid-fifties, Europe underwent changes in every domain (mechanization of agriculture, development of transportation, expansion of the automobile industry). As a result of war destruction, new factories with some of the most up-to-date equipment were constructed, bringing about mass production of consumer products. All this created what has been called the "New Europe."

Today, there are still those who assume that educational changes are not necessary since this extraordinary economic expansion proves that the Common Market countries have always had at their disposal, at any level, the skilled labor necessary for expansion. But one must point out that Europe no longer benefits as was the case at the end of World War II, from the external contribution of qualified personnel formed, for example, in Germany by the refugees coming from the Eastern European countries and East Germany. As for France, Belgium, the Netherlands, and Great Britain, they benefitted from the return to the "metropole" of highly qualified professionals who had settled down in former colonies.

Well-informed observers of the European scene point out that the need for more highly qualified personnel was felt around 1955. At that time it also became clear that the educational expansion was past the point of no return for reasons we have outlined in Chapter 1.

In his article on the European school system, Fabio Luca Cavazza, referring to the mid-fifties, points out that:

At that point school administrators, scholars, and politicians began clearly to see the problem of the schools as a general political problem. Called upon to satisfy an ever increasing number of collective needs, the state had to concern itself above all with the continuity of economic development. Regardless of any change in political ideology, the state was compelled to augment the recruitment for its own leading classes, for in a world characterized by ever growing productivity and increasing organization of work, it felt the need to increase productivity in its own services and thus the qualifications of its own leading class. The particular problems of some countries accentuated the need of those governments to intervene in the formation of a larger leading class, and therefore to devote a larger part of the national income to educational services. Consider, for example, the problems that Italy has had to face in the modernization and industrialization of the south — problems that it could not solve without stimulating the creation of a new and large group of leaders. . . . In brief, the state on the one hand and industrial expansion on the other increased the rhythm of growth of the European educational structure, giving to it that impulse which was almost completely lacking between the two world wars. The European petty and middle bourgeoisie no longer have enough children to sustain in an almost exclusive manner, as they did until the immediate postwar period, the growth and turnover of the leading classes.[10]

Furthermore, especially since the close of the Second World War, economists for various reasons have manifested an increasing interest in the problems of education, emphasizing the relationship between education and economic planning. As a matter of fact, European educators, economists, and planning experts have been among the most attentive observers of the conditions required for economic expansion, more particularly through the Organization for Economic Cooperation and Development (OECD) which states: "In a complex industrial society, economic strength derives from technology — in particular, the application of science and industry. This in turn is based on the creative capacity of man and his education."

Already in 1958, Pierre Harmel, then Belgian Minister of Justice, could state:

Any valuable effort for the extension of studies has, today, an investment value. The social economic expansion is from now on a tributary of the development of education. The obstacles put to the growth of the school restrain the development of prosperity. The testimonies in this sense coming from all parts of the world are explicit. More than money, more than the resources of the earth and of nature, the quality of human resources, prepared in time so as to correspond to the social needs of ten or fifteen years later, is the dominant element in continuous economic progress and the increase of the standard of living.[11]

One finds the same affirmations in Great Britain with Lord Beveridge, in France in the Longchambon report and with Jean Fournastie, and in Switzerland with Jaccard. Moreover, "after a civilization based for centuries upon the richness of the land, we are leaving a second economic state based upon material wealth and coming to a more dignified period which will base its expansion on intellectual wealth."[12]

New economic theories, industrial expansion, the development of the "third sector," and the impossibility for the traditional leading classes to fully provide the new leadership is, then the background against which must be seen the new measures applied in education which we presented previously, giving in part satisfaction to the democratic principles laid down twenty years earlier by Langevin-Wallon but bringing about a difficult choice for those "democratic" forces advocating most strongly the application of the Langevin-Wallon principles: either the struggle for a university withdrawn within itself, living in a closed world, which one will try to protect against pressures from private economic sectors judged to be interested in quick results; or, on the contrary, to contribute indirectly to the creation of a university submitted to economic interests. This choice is then represented by the alternative: liberal university – technocratic university.

The demands of the students and professorial associations were concerned with budget, which seemed to have magic virtues and would allow the solution the pressing problems caused by the increase in the number of students. This increase had resulted in lack of space and professors. "Premises and professors" became the slogan. There are many who believe that if satisfaction were given to the material demands, the quality of education would increase and the number of students failing the examinations would diminish. Maurice Duverger has been a strong supporter of these proposed measures, and he recently completed an experiment at the Faculte de Droit in which a number of students received more attention from a greater number of assistant professors. The result was that less failures were to be counted among these "temporarily privileged" students.

Such measures, referring to the material tasks of higher education and the financial means to carry them out properly and quickly, and not to a profound restructuring of the university, have been the battle ground for academics and students. Indeed, in reaction to the outside attacks against university traditionalism and incapacity to adapt to the modern world, the position of the academics was and still is defensive.

In France, for example, the annual meeting of the National Union of Higher Education (Syndicat National de l'Enseignement Superieur) which ended on April 24, 1966, stated in its final resolution, referring to the Fouchet reform of higher education, that it would not propose a counter-reform "which can be deformed by the government at will," and reiterated its hostility toward the "principles and conditions of elaboration" of the reform Fouchet. The Secretary General of the Union, Mr. Legay, stated that "all the countries of the world undergo in their educational structures the enormous shock provoked by economic and scientific expansion. The technocrats have made a slight advance, but they have not won. . . ."

And in its manifesto, "The Answer of the University," published in April, 1964, the same union stated that the "present crisis is not essentially due to the weaknesses of the structures, but to the lack of means." This opinion is contradictory to that expressed by the students (during these last few years only) demanding a restructuring of the university:

Internal transformation of Higher Education: With respect to the subject matter of education, the requirements which we formulate in the methods and structures correspond to the necessities of a formation centered on professional training: education must permit the acquisition of a certain number of studies corresponding to actual developments of the science and techniques, while having a polyvalent character, in order to prepare for the reconversion which will be rendered necessary by the ulterior evolution of science (especially by the introduction of a methodological formation). Finally, the unitarian university with diverse internal structures, refusing all numerus clausus [quota systems] seem to us the only reply to the objectives which we fix for it.[13]

Without any doubt the measures already carried out or being considered at present, with regard to the secondary school systems, will bring about an increase in the number of graduates at the secondary school level, which remains the main preparation to higher studies. These graduates can then, if they wish, follow tradition and enroll in the university. We have seen that up to now the great majority of European "Bacheliers" chose to do so. It is true that, to a certain extent, more particularly in the Netherlands and Germany, a stagnation in the percentage of secondary school graduates entering the university can be foreseen in the near future. One cannot with certainty forecast that this trend will be generalized from 1972 onward — at that date the children entering secondary school today under the new measures will graduate. What will happen then if this great number of graduates seek entrance into the university? Or will they enter professional life?

The economic factor. Planning experts, educators, politicians, and leading figures in business and industry do not hide their fear of seeing a great number of students enter the university, pursue costly and long studies, and create perhaps erroneous views about the "brilliant" future that is promised to those who finish their university studies. Will that brilliant future not be hard, unsatisfactory, and requiring not at all the type of qualifications these university graduates have received? In other words, one expects a problem of employment for those highly qualified and cultured individuals. This poses, then, the problem of orientation in terms of the possibilities of the employment market. "The task is," says Raymond Poignant, a French planning expert, "to seek the optimum correlations between jobs and types and level of training and to define the norms of training in the different branches of the national economy." Another element to be considered is that these correlations and norms are not static and are subject to change as a result of the evolution of technology. Orientation? Yes, but what will be the criteria by which one orients this particular child to the university and the other to a technical school? Even if this orientation does not have to be authoritarian, factors such as the establishment of new schools, the opening of new sections within the existing schools, counseling of students and their parents . . . can have in themselves an orientating power. The danger remains that the higher social classes will, by nature, elect for their children that type of education offering the greatest esteem and future possibilities.

The social factor. Although it would be desirable to determine the type of training that is needed, both for the economy and for the aspiring individual, can one rightfully rule out the spontaneous desires of the individual wanting to reach the highest levels of knowledge that his capacities allow? Some scholars solve this problem temporarily by pointing out that the need for "cadres" in the Common Market countries is so great that the point of saturation for the highly qualified university trained professional will not come for quite a while. And in any case, they say, the IUT in France and the non-university institutes of technical training in the other countries will respond to the desires of a large number of students.

Frequently, one refers to the United States, where a great number of individuals finish secondary education and even college without creating problems at the employment level. The same can be said for the Soviet Union. On a long-term basis, it might be quite possible that the development of secondary schools and higher education go beyond the needs of the economy in terms of the accepted definition of the type of training that is needed for a particular type of job. But, says Poignant, "such a perspective is the consequence and the result of the democratization policy with regard to access to prolonged studies and there is nothing that could possibly be a matter of worry with regard to employment possibilities." The basis of this reasoning is that the history of all the advanced industrial societies shows that there is a constant increase in the kind of training one has to receive to qualify for the same type of job. Degradation of studies? If at the secondary level — where there is no particular specialization — the increase in the number of graduates might not become a major problem, and if one does accept that more studies will be necessary to occupy a post for which fifty years ago only low and short training period was necessary, the same cannot be said for the university where education prepared the individual for a very highly specialized type of profession. Is it then conceivable that one will permit a student to enter the university to pursue long studies directed toward a profession in which society's demands are satisfied?

Reaction of the University

Faced with an expected continuous increase in the number of students, and equally concerned with the accompanying economic, social, and pedagogical problems, a tendency toward "selection" for entrance into the university is appearing in European university circles. It is stimulated by the great percentage of failures at the examinations, particularly in the first year of the university, and is advocated in the name of the quality of higher education and of democratization: "no selection without democratization, no democratization without selection," says French mathematician and professor at the University of Paris, Laurent Schwartz.

Opposition to selective entrance stemmed, and still does stem, from a scrupulous respect for the traditional liberalism permitting entrance into the university to every graduate of secondary school, from the unsatisfactory democratization of the secondary level, and from the fear that selection at the university level might be as unfavorable toward lower social classes as was the secondary school. Opposition also stems from the non-existence or insufficient existence of a different type of higher education than that offered by the university. Today, however, with the great increase in the number of pupils at the secondary school level, the democratization of studies, and the creation of various institutions of higher learning other than the university, the question is openly discussed by university leaders. It finds a favorable reaction in governmental, industrial, and business milieu for reasons we previously outlined and which mainly concern the need, on a short-term basis at least, for medium professionals.

It seems, then, that the question is no longer whether selection is necessary, but at what level it will take place and what the possibilities are for those who have been refused entrance. We will consider here the various discussions or measures that have been taken in the countries considered regarding the selection process.

In Belgium the law of June 8, 1964, decreeing the "polyvalence" of all secondary school degrees, also lays out the organization of "maturity examinations" to be taken at the end of secondary school. They are fully applicable for the first time from the present academic year onwards, i.e., in July, 1966, upon graduation from secondary school, those who wish to apply for entrance into the university must pass the "maturity examination." It consists of a dissertation eventually followed by a discussion with the examiners on the subject of the dissertation and an oral examination on one principal subject matter or two secondary subject matters. According to Van Mele, Belgian Ministry of Education official, approximately 10 percent of the candidates who had presented themselves at this examination in 1965 did not succeed. It was not then compulsory but could be taken by those who sought the "polyvalence" of their secondary school degree, although the result did not disqualify the candidates for entrance into the university. As we have pointed out, "polyvalence" is a step toward democratization of higher education. At the same time, the selective potentialities of the maturity examination seem to be considerable, since the requirements of this examination can be increased in the years to come while keeping the requirements for secondary studies' degrees at such a level that many students will be able to attend these courses and obtain the degrees. Thus they satisfy the needs of the national economy for medium professionals who receive a basic culture at school and are trained in their profession in the company for which they work.

In the Netherlands and Italy no measures for selective entrance into the University have as yet been taken. But discussions about differentiating higher education have been going on for quite a number of years, particularly in the Netherlands where the creation of the "baccalaureaat" has been considered since 1949. And by definition, differentiation of higher education makes a selection system necessary, which presupposes an orientation cyclus.

While the Italian Commission, when suggesting differentiation of higher education, stressed the necessity for "efficiency" of higher education and for the solving of the problem of the medium professionals, Dutch scholars seemed to find the justification for differentiation of higher education in the development of science and the accompanying specialization of academics. More particularly, they point out the consequences of this high specialization for teaching in the earlier years of higher education. One must remember here that, following the German example (Humboldt), higher education in the Netherlands is based upon the unity of research and teaching, "but only for as long as science formed a unity in itself could its identification with both teaching and research benefit both elements of education."[14]

Today, however, according to Dutch scholars, because of the development of science, the thesis of unity of both teaching and research can be upheld only in the last years of higher education at which time students have already received a basic training and can follow from then on with the greatest benefit a training for researchers. They also point out that if this trend continues without a basic change within the university, higher education may become a research institute only and cut itself off from younger and first-year students, thus losing its soul.

With this perspective and the Anglo-Saxon example in mind, where research and teaching find their unity only from the graduate level on, preceded by a three- or four-year course of general studies with little or no training for research, Dutch scholars believe that one of the best solutions both for students and professors on the one hand, and for quality of education and development of science on the other hand, lies in the creation of a "baccalaureaat."

The aim is to remain faithful to the duty towards general culture – this not only to serve science but also to serve *man* and not only for the benefit of his intellectual capacities. Not professional academic training in the prescribed form of science, with concepts in certain specialized domains, but education based on teaching of a certain 'savoir vivre' giving the academician the capacity of finding his own way in the society and facing problems of every day. This is the ideal to be attained. Only the best will be chosen for further study, only those who go independently towards scientific research.

For those who do not qualify for science, three or four years of education is sufficient. For them it is better to obtain an inferior academic degree and look for a job in the society: further studies will not serve any purpose. The university gets the best of students as soon as the "mass" leaves, and at that moment it is possible to devote oneself only to the best students. The society is also taking advantage of these two branches of the higher education system. First of all, academic candidates are placed quickly and in a large number at the society's disposal and they can occupy immediately situations among the guiding classes, and they have at the same time possibilities in educating their successors, i.e., the new generation. This concept of education is not concentrated on science but on the education of a certain type of person and has given the university a large possibility of adapting to an upcoming democratic system.[15]

In Germany, where, as we have seen, reforms of the secondary school have been limited up to now to offering the possibility of switching from one section to another in the course of study (although the idea of some kind of "tronc commun" has been considered), the idea that only 3 to 4 percent of an age group have the necessary aptitudes for attending the university is still widespread, as notes Professor Friedrich Edding (Institute for International Research in Education, Frankfort). And since, for a few years now, the number of students has been higher than this percentage, many think the increase in the rate of attendance is a mistaken investment. The Council for Higher Education and Research – Wissenschaftsrat – does not share this opinion, but does question whether one will not soon reach the stage of decreasing efficiency, particularly if the rate of admission continues to increase as it did in the last ten years.

But Professor Edding responds easily to this question by a comparison with other countries of Western Europe, where 10 percent or more of an age group succeed in the final examination of secondary studies: why then should a percentage of five to six be considered too much in Germany? Furthermore, in the United States and the Soviet Union, 10 percent of the students of an age group succeed in their examinations after four to six years of higher studies, and there is then no reason to think that 10 percent of an age group *starting* higher education would inevitably bring with it a decrease in quality. "It seems the problem is not so much the reserve of intelligence, but more the appropriate methods for development of these aptitudes. The following statistics show that the percentage of dropouts from secondary school is quite considerable (Table 2-10). Is this indispensable to maintaining the level of quality or for other reasons? To answer such a question would require a great deal of empirical research."[16]

The second conference of European Universities' Rectors (presidents) and vice-presidents stated:

The requirements of the society are so high that the university has to meet new responsibilities by taking care that a maximum of qualified people are sent out, which means education of a large number of average level students at the same time as education of highly qualified students on an academic basis. Consequently, the university cannot have a fixed educational system but has to take into consideration several education systems adapted to different standards. This is already done in several countries, but in practice many problems are still unsolved.[17]

The "Wissenschafstrat" is at present studying the possibilities of orientation for those who want to pursue their studies in different directions from those offered by the university, as much on the secondary school level as on the higher education level. Indeed, the students attending the secondary school have, generally speaking, only two choices: either they succeed in their examinations and then judge it necessary to pursue their studies at the university; or they do not succeed, in which case they drop out of school, usually after the sixth year of study. In this latter case they are considered more or less as failures. Members of the "Wissenschafstrat" believe that it would be desirable to give some kind of degree to those students who abandon secondary school studies. Furthermore, it is investigating the possibilities of secondary school graduates finding suitable positions in society, in which case the secondary school degree would not be considered only as the beginning of (higher) studies but also as the end of a complete cyclus of studies. This would then dissuade youngsters from going to the universities, especially when these youngsters are not really interested in pursuing a higher education but choose that direction because of the limited alternative possibilities that secondary school graduation opens to them and because of the traditional role of secondary schools studies. Prof. Edding, however, adds that this thinking responds less to a desire to diminish the number of students wishing to attend the university than to the desire to prevent too many failures in the course of studies. "The principal goal is to avoid waste." Another proposition put to the Wissenschaftsrat, for the same reasons as were involved for secondary education, is the creation of some kind of intermediary degree obtainable after a number of years of higher studies, half way between

58

Table 2-10

Federal Republic of Germany: Enrollment Rate of Students Born in 1942 in
the Lycees During Eight Academic
Years

Age	11	12	13	15	16	17	18	*Percentage of decrease between the yr. of highest & 1960/61*
Schleswig-Hostein	12.5	13.5	12.8	12.8	11.6	9.8	8.4	38
Hamburg	12.5	5.2	14.0	13.3	11.6	9.7	7.9	44
Lower Saxony	9.9	11.2	11.5	11.0	10.7	9.8	8.5	26
Bremen	0.0	5.0	14.4	14.6	13.1	11.8	10.2	30
Westphalia-North Rhineland	12.9	14.0	13.7	12.3	11.1	9.5	7.6	46
Hesse	15.7	17.8	18.2	16.6	15.2	12.8	10.7	41
Rhineland-Palatinate	14.6	15.6	15.3	13.0	11.2	9.1	7.7	51
Baden-Wurttenberg	17.4	19.2	18.5	16.5	14.0	10.0	8.7	54
Bavaria	7.3	15.3	15.8	12.8	11.3	9.5	7.9	50
Territory of Saar	7.3	15.3	15.8	11.3	9.9	8.6	7.1	50
Federal Republic	12.3	14.6	15.1	13.4	12.0	10.0	8.2	45
West Berlin	1.3	15.1	19.1	17.4	15.8	13.7	11.9	38

entrance to the university and the final examinations. Too many students abandon their studies in courses, receiving no proof whatever of their time spent at the university, while others pursue their studies thanks only to an enormous desire to finish their studies, although they have very often lost interest.[18]

It is generally understood in Germany that the structure of the employment market is more differentiated than that of higher education. "It seems to me that education must make a great effort to adapt itself, and, in this sense, one might consider the creation of a partial degree as a step forward in this direction."[19] Furthermore, the Wissenschaftsrat hopes to orient a number of students wanting to pursue higher education toward other institutions of higher learning. The Wissenschafstrat wants to obtain an even more pronounced differentiation, believing that a great number of students presently attending the university will benefit more from a more professionally oriented type of education. But one must observe that it will be difficult to obtain substantial results in this direction, especially because of ·the prestige linked to a university education.

These preoccupations of the Wissenschafstrat, deal with those students attending the secondary school whose parents have decided, when their child is at ten or twelve years of age, that the child will eventually pursue higher education. We have seen which factors come into the making of this decision anywhere in Europe. And in spite of the assertions of Prof. Edding, a member of the Wissenschaftsrat, that these preoccupations have not as an object limitations of entrance into the university, but are concerned with "waste" and the consequent suggestion to create an intermediary degree, both at the secondary school level and at the university level, they seem to us to stem from a desire for "selectivity."

If one considers the various possibilities offered in Germany by professional and technical educational institutions, it seems quite unnecessary to create intermediary degrees at both secondary and higher educational level. On one hand, there is a problem of orientation at a very early stage of education; i.e., upon entrance into the secondary school; and on the other hand, great difficulties for political, economic, (teachers) and psychological reasons, that do not permit at this time to install an orientation, although the principle has been adopted. In other words, the Wissenschaftsrat does not seem to be willing to run up against the desire of the family to send its children to secondary school even if they are not fit for this type of study and eventually will drop out. This is true even if the child receives some kind of a degree testifying to his attendance at secondary school or university — or will it testify·to his failure?

In France, expansion of higher education, as we have seen, has been considerable and the new measures taken regarding secondary school will have, as a direct result, an increase in the number of individuals seeking entrance into the university. It was seriously considered at the time of elaboration of the reforms. However, knowing the opposition of the students and of a large percentage of professors to the selective entrance system, Minister Fouchet has not violated the liberal tradition with respect to this matter. The "official" justification for a selective entrance system was, as in Germany, to seek a greater quality and to avoid waste — based again upon the high percentage of students who either stop their studies after one or two years, or double or even triple the years of the cyclus.

However, there is within the university itself a great tendency among academics to consider a selective system. Even Prof. Jean-Marie Legay, Faculty of Sciences, University of Lyon, and Secretary General of one of the more radical professorial unions (Syndicat National de l'Enseignement Superieur), declares: "I'm not an enemy of selection. But I do discuss the conditions in which it would take place. If it was up to me it should be done in the course of the first year (of the university), perhaps even during the first six months." Through examinations? Professors' decisions? The problem has not yet been studied that far. Prof. Zamansky, Dean of the Faculty of Sciences of the University of Paris, says: "I would like to have the right to refuse secondary school graduates . . . by their student career and age, and by obliging them to take an entrance examination. But even those who "flunked" at the baccalaureat could present themselves by individual decision and upon a dossier for this entrance examination." In November, 1965, Prof. Zamansky had asked for the creation of an entrance examination. The proposition was approved by the assembly of professors, but judged unacceptable by an administrative court.

In France, where the IUT will open, the problem of selection, i.e., who will go where, is primary. Minister Fouchet was not at all clear on this particular subject. Moreover, over the last ten years at least, it has become more and more evident that admission to higher education in the countries considered is not necessarily decided at the moment of entrance into the university. In the strict sense, entrance into the university has for centuries been decided chiefly at the primary school level. Now, with the extension of the period of compulsory school attendance and the expansion of secondary education and, particularly in Italy, with the establishment of the "tronc commun," the decision can be taken half-way through secondary studies, and in Belgium at the end of secondary school through the "maturity examination." In France and Belgium respectively the first year with the application of the reforms, perhaps after completion of two years of study, and the first two years (candidature — the word itself indicates well that these two years constitute really a candidature to higher education) are the levels where selections essentially take place. As Prof. Frank Bowles, director of the international study on admission into the university (under the sponsorship of UNESCO and IAU), remarks, systems of this nature (propedeutique, candidature . . .) reduce the number of students entering the higher cyclus by 30 to 50 percent. In France the rate of success at the first level varies from 45 to 60 percent, whereas for Belgium the rate of success in 1959-60 was, after the first year, for Letters 39 percent, for Science 40 percent. As such, then, notes Prof. Bowles, one should consider these examinations as "advanced entrance examinations."

"Since the war, admission selection has moved from the entrance to the secondary school to selection at the university for higher training. This, as in

U.S. graduate and professional school entrance exams, will lead to continually higher norms of admission."

Will the same changes intervene in the European system, installing what has been called the "numerus clausus" and abandoning the liberal system. There are factors supporting this supposition as we have seen. But the main difficulty is the criterion which will be taken into consideration. Here we touch the problem of orientation which in France, for example, has been the object of various propositions with respect to organization and the period needed for orientation.

This assertion leads to reconsideration of the organization of secondary education. One will, eventually discover that the two concepts of democratization — democratization of institutions and democratization of studies — ought not to be contradictory, but complementary.

Indeed, it seems that only a democratization of studies, through the creation of a "tronc commun" for a period of three years in which orientation could take place in the most equitable way possible with an appropriate program of study (which will require for the years to come a number of experiments and considerable pedagogical research), will diminish the influence of social and economic factors. The next step, then, would be the democratization of institutions as was proposed and outlined previously.

When thinking of this problem of organization of secondary schools and of orientation, one remark made by the Langevin-Wallon commission constantly comes to mind: "Culture is what unites men, professions are what most separate them."

3   Planning and Finances

The world, which man is constructing in the 20th century of rapidly growing scientific knowledge and technical development without precedence, is in constant evolution. While only a short time ago one could safely assume that social and economic structures would last for at least a generation, today they seem in constant flux. The rapidity of change gives little time to understand a given social dynamic. In this growing complexity man continues his drive to know and control the factors of change.

Nowhere is this more apparent than in education, where the product goes five years or so into an unknown future while created in an institution still heavily tied to the past by tradition and habit. This then provides the impetus as well as the problems for the planners.

One of France's greatest authorities in educational planning, Raymond Poignant, remarks that:

> drawing up an educational development plan does not mean trying to define an ideal . . ., but more modestly making a practical study of what the authorities can do to promote education within a given period of time — usually four to five years. This means determining needs (for facilities and teachers) in relation to medium-term educational targets or forecasts, established not in the abstract but in terms of a great many practical realities, and in particular knowing that the resources sought for education have to be weighed against other national needs and that discriminating between these needs, which is the very essence of planning, can be the responsibility only of the highest national authorities, i.e., Government and Parliament.[1]

How to Define the Needs

To define needs one must first evaluate the evolution in the number of individuals attending school at all levels of the educational system (primary, secondary, university, technical schools, etc.). This is one of the more difficult tasks of the planning commission which has to evaluate very carefully the various factors which influence the number of individuals who will attend school over the next planning period and beyond.

The factors we set forth previously with regard to the increase in the number of students have here again to be taken into consideration and analyzed, not to explain the increase but to forecast it. The first factor which has to be taken into account is demography.

The demographic situation. Birth rate is naturally the basis of any forecasting of the number of children who will be attending school. As long as one takes this into consideration for primary school, there is no complex problem of calculation. However, one should note here *social mobility,* or the phenomena of urbanization. In most countries population is concentrated around the cities, changing considerably the school map of the European countries.

But it is not sufficient to take into consideration only the present demographic evolution. One must also put forth hypotheses with regard to birth rates in the years to come, although this is less important with regard to higher education into which individuals enter at the age of twenty, leaving thus a period of twenty years for the public powers to take the necessary measures. This is true at least for building requirements. But one should also note the necessity for training teachers for a growing or prospectively growing student population.

The social demand. This is a very difficult factor to analyze since it corresponds to a spontaneous desire of parents and children to attend school for a longer period of time. For the countries of the Common Market the question is, at this time, the entrance of students into secondary school, which is the next step in social evolution, and desire for education, but ultimately it will reach, as it already does in the United States, higher education. Previously we have noted the marked differences in this social demand resulting from the social and geographic origin of the student (agricultural areas, linguistic origin, as in Belgium), which poses serious problems, in particular with respect to the development of a particular area of the country (for example, Southern Italy). By social origin we do not only mean the financial situation of the family, but also the cultural traditions of the family, or of a region. But what appears to be most important for planners with regard to the social demand factor is evaluation of the evolution of this spontaneous reaction of the individual toward education. Raymond Poignant points out the importance of the time factor in the development of the educational system. It is indeed impossible to elaborate plans which do not correspond to economic and social evolution. At certain moments of educational history there appear sudden expanded consciousness on the part of the population, which increases considerably, over a short period of time, the enrollment at all levels of education. This time factor is of crucial importance to planners, and could be determined and analyzed on the basis of sociological studies.

Democratization of education. The consequences of the trends described in Chapter 2 are of the greatest importance for planners as we have pointed out in great detail. We will not come back to this aspect here.

Educational needs for economic and social development. In recent years economists and policy makers have expressed their interest in the relationship of education and economic growth, claiming, on the one hand, that economic growth "constitutes the fundamental motor of development of education." Economic growth and rising standards of living seem to create material and psychological conditions permitting an extension of education; prolonged education can be considered as a particular type of consumption, increasing as the standard of living increases. But, on the other hand, the degree of skill and knowledge that a work force possesses contributes to its productivity. As technical development progresses, liberating man from menial tasks, a higher level of qualification of the working force makes it necessary, since techniques change rapidly, to posess of a large general culture so as to enable the individual to adapt himself to the changing requirements of technology. The conclusion is, then, that educational development is at the same time a condition and a consequence of economic development.

From this point of view, education is considered by modern economists as an investment. The necessity for educating a future labor force so as to satisfy a growing economy and a changing technology has brought with it attempts to define the "needs" of the economy and to introduce this notion of needs into the educational development plan. "The problem of satisfying economic needs for qualified personnel has in recent years and in many countries become the motive or pretext for a sudden wave of interest in the planned development of school systems."[2]

There are some objections formulated with regard to this "manpower needs" approach to the development of education, and Philip H. Coombs refers to the new versus the traditional concept of the role of education:

It is well to note that there is potentially a serious philosophical conflict between this new manpower interest in education and the traditional view of education's role in a free society. In the context of the 'manpower shortage,' the educational system comes to be viewed as a 'brain power industry' whose social function is to develop human beings as instruments for building national economic and military strength. Under the older view, it was taken for granted that education contributed indirectly to the economic and general welfare of the nation, but the overarching purpose of education in a free society was to enable individuals to realize their full human potentialities for their own sake.[3]

The national "pool of ability." With present trends in the development of secondary and higher education it is believed that the growth of educational systems in their present form can be limited only by the individual's ability to benefit from education. It is accepted, however, that no country has, as yet, reached this "point of maturity." But, as Raymond Poignant points out:

It would be wrong to think that this question of the ceiling on intellectual capacity is of no importance for our current educational forecasting. On the contrary, in many countries the reform of secondary education is prompting inquiries to determine the maximum percentage of children in a given age group who can profit from a general secondary education. In this particular case the question of the ceiling on capacity becomes an important factor in estimating the resources needed to carry out such reforms.[4]

We shall now proceed to present the methods used for the elaboration of a plan for educational development in different countries, introducing each section with the reply given by the country dealt with to the International Inquiry of the International Bureau of Education in 1962.[5]

The Netherlands

To the fundamental question of the International Bureau of Education inquiry, "Does educational planning exist in your country?" the Dutch government replied with a preliminary note pointing out that:

as various meanings may be given to the concept of planning . . . the word is taken (here) to mean the line of conduct followed with a view to planning rather than actual planning . . . . in conformity with the above definition it is possible in the Netherlands to speak of a system of educational planning. Scientific research is employed more and more in the drawing up of plans. So far it has not been a question of integral planning, although the development is undoubtedly tending in that direction.[6]

It is doubtful that this clarifies the situation, although one can conclude that the Dutch government, with great precaution, claims to possess some kind of education plan or planning. However, we will not enter into a discussion of their concept of planning, but will accept the careful wording of the formula adopted in the recommendation of the 1962 International Conference on Public Education (Geneva):

While proclaiming the principle of autonomy and cultural independence of each country and the necessity of national education plans inspired out of the experience and the problems pertaining to each of them, it is important to underline the value of an international cooperation in favor of educational planning which recognizes at the same time the existence of various conceptions in this matter and the interest in being able to go to various fountainheads to recruit qualified experts and obtain authorized advice.

For the purpose of this study, we too reserve our judgment on the concept of planning and associate ourselves with the scruples of the conference delegates. We will thus proceed to a presentation of the present functioning of the forecasting of educational development in the Netherlands, as well as in the other countries considered.

Law on higher education.   The Higher Education Act (Jan. 1, 1961) provides in its article 97 that universities (public and private) elaborate every four years a development scheme (official translation of the Dutch "ontwikkelingsplannen") which they present to the Ministry of Education and Science and to the Academic Council which examines them as a whole and sends its judgment to the Minister of Education and Science and to the Minister of Agriculture.

Mission, composition and working methods of the Academic Council. Created by the new Higher Education Act, the very existence of the Academic Council testifies to the willingness to consider and treat higher education as a whole, with particular reference to the private IHL. Indeed, the principle that equal opportunities for development should be offered to public and private universities alike is based on the idea that the interests of higher education and scientific research can be entrusted to public and private universities, stimulating unity of higher education in the Netherlands which should also stimulate cooperation between the various universities and ease the financial burden of higher education.

The Academic Council is meant to function as a link between the universities themselves and between the universities and the society (i.e., governmental bodies). The Council encourages collaboration between the universities and tends to promote the adaptation of higher education to the development of science and to the requirements of society. It is considered essential that there exist a coordinating body to evaluate the problems from a national point of view and to make recommendations to the government and the universities accordingly.

As mentioned already, the universities' schemes are submitted to the Academic Council which considers these schemes as a whole and advises the Minister on such matters as to whether the future policy of each individual university fits into the general policy for higher education and research.

The Academic Council consists of a chairman, appointed by the Crown, two members from each university, one of whom is appointed every year by the Senate (body composed of the rector and at least four professors of various faculties, whose main duty is to safeguard the general interests of education and research), and the other by the board of curators (governmental body of the university dealing with accommodation and financial administration). With the exception of the professors and lecturers, it appoints the whole staff. The Crown appoints the Board of Curators (in the case of state universities), and ten non-university members, nominated by the Council and appointed by the Crown.

In accordance with the authority given it by the Higher Education Act, the Academic Council has set up approximately twenty commissions corresponding to the most important university disciplines and several study groups (permanent and ad hoc). Both the study groups and the commissions are composed of experts who are not necessarily members of the Council.

The first development plans elaborated by the universities cover the period 1963-66. We now present the main characteristics of these plans.

Preliminary remarks. The development schemes have not been elaborated in terms of specific directions, since Dutch authorities estimate that the first development schemes themselves would, at best, demonstrate what the future schemes should contain so as to give the necessary insight and make valuable comparisons possible. But Article 97, paragraph 3 of the Higher Education Act stipulates that directives should leave the necessary freedom as to enable each university to give its own mark to the schemes. These schemes are not limited to any specific period and, as a matter of fact, one of the universities went beyond 1966 with its development scheme, nor do they have the characteristics of a precise program which has to respect a specific time schedule.

Forecasting the numbers of students in terms of the demographic evolution and economic and social factors. The increase of the number of students is studied by a central bureau, the Central Bureau of Statistics, which completed a first study in 1959 indicating that by 1970 Dutch university enrollment would be 64,500 and the number of first-year students would reach 10,500. The first development schemes of the universities have been elaborated on the basis of these 1959 estimates. However, in November, 1964, the Central Bureau of Statistics, completing a second study with regard to student increase up to 1970, estimates that the total number of students in the Netherlands will be 80,130 and the figure for first-year students is 11,650. This anticipated increase in the number of students is now considered as real because the Central Bureau of Statistics elaborated its statistics on the known figures of higher secondary school enrollment. The Bureau also indicated the evolution of the number of students by institutions and fields of study. On demand of the Academic Council, the Central Bureau of Statistics and the bureaus of statistics of the various IHL will from now on maintain close contacts.

The discrepancy of almost 25 percent between the forecasts of 1959 and 1964 seems to be due to the increasing interest in the exact sciences, bringing with it a longer period of study and also the change in secondary school studies. However, the increase in the forecast does not seem to be accounted for by a relative increase in the number of students passing from secondary school to higher education.

Economic and social factors. The Central Bureau of Statistics has also undertaken studies to evaluate the needs and possibilities of employment for the graduates of certain fields of study, i.e., medicine, letters, and technical sciences. With respect to the latter, the need for engineers had previously (1959) been calculated on the basis of the relationship between the needs for engineers and the increase in production in the Netherlands, which was assumed to increase by 3 percent annually. Today experts estimate that the production increase will be higher than 3 percent and, consequently, the need for engineers will be increasing. If there will be a further increase of the rate of growth of production of 1 percent per annum, the need for engineers in 1980 would be 20 percent higher than the previous estimate. The Central Bureau is scheduled to complete its forecast of future needs and it is expected that they will have risen sharply.

Among factors which, according to Minister Diepenhorst, will influence the development of the number of students attending the university is demographic evolution. New forecasting studies have been undertaken showing an increase in the population because of changes in the age of marriage and less emmigration; the expected increase in per capita income will stimulate social demand and influence enrollment in secondary schools as well as stimulate a greater demand for services (more particularly doctors, lawyers, etc.). There is in almost every sector of industry a reorganization of production methods in view of increasing production (the Dutch economy is best characterized as an economy of manufacturing) which will be accompanied by a greater demand for university trained professionals (business administration, production methods, etc.).

Dutch authorities had hoped that great publicity given to the needs and possibilities of employment in a particular field would orient students in their choice of studies. But a study by the Central Planning Bureau has shown that the effects were minute. New effects of orientation, mainly through larger publicity, will be attempted.

Material problems. The increasing interest in higher education, the growth of population, and the increasing demand for university graduates in all branches of human activity require the construction of new buildings and the creation of totally new institutions. This is particularly true for medicine (a seventh faculty of medicine will be created) and the technical IHL to which priority is given in the frame of the policy of industrialization pursued by the Netherlands (a fourth technical institution of higher learning will be created).

With regard to teaching personnel, the Academic Council decided in November, 1963, to institute an ad hoc commission to study this problem in terms of the development plans presented by the universities. This commission studies whether it is possible, through defining and analyzing the factors which condition the need for teaching personnel, to elaborate a general method for evaluation of the total demands for teaching personnel which would also indicate the necessary ratios between the numbers of professors, lecturers, "charge de cours," scientific assistants and students.

From the development plans presented by the universities for the period 1963-66, one can extract three main points: development of specialization, division of tasks, cooperation between the various universities (state and private).

Because of the growing differentiation of science, the universities, in their development plans, generally claim that it is neither desirable nor necessary that all the universities be fully equipped for every branch of science and every specialization. Without giving a clear and complete answer on how they would deal with such a division of tasks, they do at least pose the question and some of them formulate some remarks.

The University of Leyden (state) states that "it is not desirable that each university tend to practice a greater number of aspects of science."[7] Leyden University's commission has presented a number of conclusions with regard to the criteria which should be taken into consideration for the creation of a new professorship (chair): when it concerns the development of a science situated on the frontier line between two faculties, regular consultations should take place between the faculties concerned. If, for reasons of greater specialization, a part of the main branch of study has to be separated from this main branch, then it is preferable to keep the central professorship (chair) and create a number of lectureships. A certain consultation is desirable when it concerns branches of study rarely practiced or hyper-specialized. The State University of Groningen states in its development plan that it will tend to favor the development of particular specialities not practiced in other universities, without hampering the development of existing branches.

One of the commissions of the Academic Council, the Commission for Social

Sciences (sociology, economy, psychology, pedagogy, cultural anthropology, and non-western sociology), believes that a small country like the Netherlands must accept limits and will be able to dedicate itself to only a small number of sciences, in terms particularly of the number and the qualifications of persons available to pursue scientific research. With regard to the creation of new professorships, this commission thinks it is preferable to nominate a greater number of scientific collaborators working under the supervision of the professor. Moreover, it estimates that the tendency to continuous specialization and the development that it brings with it in other sectors (personnel, investments, laboratories, etc.) must be qualified in the sense that each university limit itself to an all-around training in the basic fields of study with only a few specializations. Although these recommendations concern the previously cited branches of study, the Academic Council and the government believe that they are of the greatest value for the other branches of study as well. The Commission recommends, in any case, a division of labor among the universities combined with increasing cooperation between the various universities. The coordination of the available assets in the universities is a necessary condition to development.

Minister of Science and Education Diepenhorst stated that although the Act of January 1, 1961, has sustained the principle of equal possibilities of development for all universities, public as well as private, necessitating increased financial means, this does not mean that the IHL can claim financial contributions from the state for all forms of specialization.

Mobility of students and professors. The Academic Council recommends very strongly interuniversity exchange of professors and students, supporting the conclusion of its Commission on the Exact Sciences. With regard to student mobility, various plans advocate that financial aid should be given to students whose training would require study of a science at some other institution than the one they normally belong to, if the chosen institution is particularly well equipped to offer this type of study. This financial aid should cover at least travel expenses and boarding, and should not be limited to especially brilliant students. However, sufficient guarantee should be presented that the money given will be spent on the type of study for which it was originally requested. Moreover, a relation could be established between the "requesting" professor and the "accepting" professor at the other university.

The various universities Commissions on the Social Sciences have stressed the importance of field trips in these branches of study (sociology, economy, psychology, etc.), considering that field research in this area is as important as research in the laboratories is for the natural sciences.

The financial plan. According to article 99, paragraph 1, the state, the private universities, and the municipal university of Amsterdam are obliged to draw up an annual financial plan estimating expenditures for the four years subsequent to the budget year. The estimates are expected to be more precise for the first and second years than for the third and fourth years. The financial plan must be based upon the four-year development plan. But for the financial plan, presented each year, the estimates "move up" a year at a time allowing adjustment of expenditures, the estimates for each new year being added successively.

The Act stipulates that upon receipt of the quadrennial financial plan submitted by the universities to the Minister of Education and Sciences, (with the reorganization of the ministry in April, 1965, the Arts sector of the Ministry has been taken over by another Ministry), the Minister of Finance shall prepare a financial plan for the whole of higher education and submit it to Parliament, together with the development schemes and financial plans drawn up by the universities. This procedure is intended to permit the Cabinet and Parliament to consider the development and the requirements of higher education, both public and private.

On July 30, 1965, the Minister of Education and Science and the Minister of Finance presented the "General Financial Plan for the Universities for the period 1966-69" to the President of the House of Representatives. It is here reproduced in Table 3-1.

Remarks. 1. The obligation for equal development possibilities makes it necessary for the government, at the moment of specifying the means to be set at the disposal of the universities, to act on the basis of norms which will be elaborated, as far as possible, in cooperation with the various institutions concerned. These norms will be gradually elaborated and will be applicable to all universities, although at the moment of application they will take the particular circumstances of the universities into consideration.

2. The above general financial plan has been submitted to the various IHL concerned before its definitive elaboration, enabling the universities to make necessary comments.

3. For calculation of personnel expenditure, both universities and government base themselves upon the existing relation between the numbers of students and professors. This student/professor ratio will be further specified in terms of the needs of each faculty from the point of view of teaching as well as of research. For the financial plan 1966-69, the following relations have been used: one professor for every twelve students in all branches of study except one for five in branches belonging to the natural sciences and mathematics and one for five in medicine, dentistry and veterinary; but with regard to this last group a correction is introduced taking into account that first-year students of these branches attend courses in mathematics and natural sciences. Furthermore, taking into consideration the necessity of disposing of a staff already well introduced to the field, when the increased number of students, in terms of which personnel number and quality have been defined, present themselves, personnel to be placed by 1969 correspond to the number of students of 1970 (see Tables 3-2 and 3-3).

Table 3-1

The Netherlands: General Financial Plan for Universities and Institutes of Higher Learning (1966-69)

	Budget			General Financial Plan f. 1,000 (1f.=$.28)		
	1964	1965	1966	1967	1968	1969
Current expenditure						
Staff expenditure	228,917	302,285	339,021	371,113	404,101	442,960
Other expenditure (excluding university hospitals)	69,948	80,524	115,867	130,350	146,644	164,975
University hospitals	49,501	66,209	72,504	79,754	87,729	96,502
Interuniversity institutes	4,775	6,503	7,653	8,598	9,675	10,888
Total current expenditure	353,141	455,521	535,045	589,815	648,149	715,325
Current revenues						
Tuition & examination fees	4,938	5,215	5,780	6,115	6,415	6,715
Other revenues	2,610	2,653	3,208	3,509	3,809	4,109
State contributions	334,839	430,071	517,751	571,000	627,845	693,460
Proper contributions and communal contributions	5,744	7,208	8,306	9,191	10,080	11,041
Balance of state contributions from preceding yr.	5,010	10,374	- -	- -	- -	- -
Total - - current revenues	353,141	455,521	535,045	589,815	648,815	715,325

| | Budget | | General Financial Plan
f. 1,000 (1f.=$.28) | | | |
	1964	1965	1966	1967	1968	1969
Capital expenditures						
Investment universities & Inst. of Higher Learning	276,073	193,811	305,184	305,211	305,211	305,211
Purchase & clearing of grounds	- - -	- - -	15,000	15,000	15,000	15,000
Expenditure on scientific research	11,210	9,800	35,000	35,000	35,000	35,000
Expansion apparatus	24,923	28,149	40,679	45,969	51,945	58,695
Total capital expenditure	312,206	231,760	395,863	401,180	407,156	413,906
Capital revenues						
State contributions	287,551	227,629	390,229	395,459	401,369	408,047
Proper contributions & communal contributions	5,495	4,131	5,634	5,721	5,787	5,859
Balance, state contribution from preceding years	19,160	- - -	- - -	- - -	- - -	- - -
Total capital revenues	312,206	231,760	395,863	401,180	407,156	413,906

Table 3-2

**The Netherlands: Evolution of the
Number of First-Year Students**
(1920/21-1970/71)

	1920/21	1937/38	1947/48	1955/56	1964/65	1970/71
Leyden	349	538	755	593	1,289	1,170
Utrecht	459	532	813	761	1,690	1,790
Groningen	155	144	239	323	1,079	1,280
Amsterdam G. U.	320	425	1,148	824	1,991	2,030
Amsterdam V. U.	44	69	154	359	935	680
Nijmegen	- -	114	158	396	1,142	1,200
Delft	439	422	1,081	940	1,622	1,550
Eindhoven	- -	- -	- -	- -	484	560
Enschede	- -	- -	- -	- -	243	450
Wageningen	65	98	154	149	411	340
Rotterdam	288	192	260	253	636	690
Tilburg	- -	57	133	109	369	510
Total	2,119	2,591	4,895	4,707	11,891	12,250

Table 3-3

The Netherlands: Evolution of the
Total Number of Students (1920/21-
1970/71)

	1920/21	1937/38	1946/48	1955/56	1964/65	1970/71
Leyden	1,344	2,384	3,553	4,294	7,314	8,820
Utrecht	1,755	2,670	4,819	5,111	9,580	12,800
Groningen	677	921	1,674	2,254	6,039	7,740
Amsterdam G. U.	1,298	2,438	5,598	6,383	11,008	13,610
Amsterdam V. U.	225	611	1,018	2,068	4,489	4,940
Nijmegen	- -	446	740	1,753	4,926	8,300
Delft	2,393	1,838	5,486	5,062	8,553	11,080
Eindhoven	- -	- -	- -	- -	2,020	3,680
Enschede	- -	- -	- -	- -	243	1,600
Wageningen	289	409	1,121	792	1,792	2,040
Rotterdam	571	566	1,225	1,296	2,762	4,410
Tilburg	- -	222	721	629	1,520	2,980
Total	8,552	12,505	25,955	29,642	60,246	82,000

Table 3-4

**The Netherlands: Public Expenditures
for Higher Education (1956-1961)**

Year	1	2	3	4
1956	129.2	4.37	29.0	31.5
1957	168.9	5.27	49.1	50.1
1958	199.6	6.16	63.1	63.1
1959	241.8	6.96	86.8	86.0
1960	286.1	7.37	104.5	101.4
1961	367.5	8.95	137.5	131.3

1. Total public expenditure in million guilders.
2. Total public expenditure expressed in 0/00 of the national revenue (market prices).
3. Investments in million guilders.
4. Investments in million guilders calculated in "prix constants" with 1958 as basis year.

Conclusion. The foregoing is a special kind of "plan," not covering a specific period in which the various measures proposed and demanded by the various planning bodies (universities, academic council, state) should be carried out. Moreover, the plan does not deal with the problem of the time of study (which seems to be getting longer and longer and which had stimulated the research toward an intermediary degree, or "baccalaureaat"). Consequently, as experience in other countries has shown (France, for example), it is doubtful that the measures proposed will be carried out within a short period of time, due to this "liberalism" with time, which apparently has permitted a greater freedom on the part of the universities to elaborate their plans. It is possible that the development of studies on the needs for manpower in a growing economy will stimulate a reorganization of higher education in the years to come, bringing with it a different type of planning, perhaps a more elaborated plan. Since the present plan does not deal with the structural reorganization of the university, one can only wonder how the democratization process will successfully be completed, with financial assistance but only minor reforms in secondary education.

Germany

In a preliminary remark to its reply to the International Bureau of Education inquiry, the Permanent Conference of Ministers of Education points out that:

It should be borne in mind that, in the Länder of the German Federal Republic and in West Berlin education from primary to university level has been organized for a long time. The advantages offered by planning are thus more limited than in countries where the education system has yet to be established. Moreover, education and therefore its planning are matters for which each state is responsible and, in order that educational development throughout the Federal Republic may be as uniform as possible, close collaboration between the Ministers of Education of the Länder constitutes part of the former's work as members of the Permanent Conference of Ministers of Education.[8]

This introduction indicates the historical and institutional difficulties that confront any effort towards planning and/or reforms in Germany, a country which, however, has to deal with serious problems — material and other — in its educational system. Indeed at the end of the Second World War, 60 percent of the school buildings were destroyed and the teaching staffs had lost many of their members. On the other hand, student enrollment at the university level kept increasing: in 1935 there were 1,091 students per one million inhabitants; in 1940, 672. But this rate increased to 2,108 in 1950, and 2,380 in 1955. The total number of students increased from about 100,000 in the early fifties to almost 200,000 by 1960, creating overcrowding of the buildings and considerably increasing the student/professor ratio. Consequently, educational expenditures increased and even the percentage of the GNP dedicated to education increased regularly, as in many other countries, but these increases were insufficient to help higher education overcome its problems and promote its expansion.[9]

This led to the creation of a central planning bureau — the Wissenschaftsrat (Council for Arts and Sciences). In 1957 the federal government and the governments of the Länder concluded an agreement and decided to cooperate within the framework of the Council, a temporary institution, the life of which was extended for five years in 1963. The Council is composed of two committees, the Academic Committee and the Administrative Committee. The Academic Committee consists of representatives of the institutions of higher education and outstanding persons nominated by the president of the Republic, and it prepares resolutions from a technical, scientific, and university point of view. The Administrative Committee considers the administrative and financial aspect of the resolutions and is composed of representatives of the Federal Government and the Länder. The Council's duties are: (1) to prepare, taking into account the suggestions of the Federal Government and the Lander, a general plan for the promotion of the arts and sciences; (2) to present a program for the execution of urgent projects; and (3) to submit recommendations for the distribution of the expenditures which the Federal government and Lander appropriate to the promotion of arts and sciences.

The Council plays a key role in the development of higher education in Germany, not so much in determining the rapidity with which expansion is brought about, which depends largely on the Länder and their financial capacities, but with regard to the general organization of higher education, this mainly because of the composition of its committees: influential academics and administrators.

However, as Prof. Friedrich Edding points out, the very creation of the

Council stimulated expenditure for higher education which by this act had received new importance.

In 1960 the Council published and presented to the president of the Republic its first report and its recommendations for the development of higher education in Germany.[10]

The Council recommended the retention (in general) of the form and spirit of the German universities, while adapting the traditions to the needs of a modern society. In particular, the Council came out strongly for maintaining the present conditions for entrance into the university: i.e., the final degree of secondary school studies, Abitur, according to Article 12 of the Constitution (Grundgesetz) guaranteeing free access to institutions of higher learning for those holding the Abitur (Abiturenten), and rejecting propositions for installing a "numerus clausus." As a result of this policy decision, an increase of teaching personnel was made necessary, and the creation of 1,200 professorial chairs and about 11,000 teaching and assistant posts was recommended.

The Council also recommended the creation of two new posts: Abteilungsvorsteher or departmental head and Wissenschaftlicher Rat (academic adviser). The holders of these posts will be involved in teaching and research and thus take off some of the pressure to which professors are subject. The departmental head will be in charge of large departments grouping various institutes, while the academic advisor will be mainly attached to faculties of liberal arts. As in Holland, the Council supports a new division of labor within the faculty, and does not plan to endow each university with a Chair for each subject of study. However, the strong individualism of the professors and the political tendencies in the various Länder have not permitted implementation of this latter recommendation. With regard to personnel, some progress has been made, but not in the proportions that the Council had recommended.

Problems with regard to the increase in the number of full professors. Various obstacles to an increase in the number of full professors are present, particularly the mode of payment. A full professor, named for life, draws besides his salary a substantial part of his income from lecture fees (Kolleggeld) which depend on the number of students attending the lecture and the subject matter. Moreover, professors enjoy complete freedom in their organization of curriculum and in the subject of their lectures. It is then understandable that many of them were reluctant to adopt new systems which would have brought about a decrease in their income, since they had to share lectures and fees with new colleagues. The Council recommended the abolition of this Kolleggeld system and negotiations have started between the professors and the Länder. So far, however, there is no substantial change.

Problems with regard to building of new faculties and modernization of existing institutions. Since present building conditions in Germany are very difficult, the construction of school buildings has suffered, and the first estimates of the cost of modernizing and expanding the existing institutions (foreseen global expenditures 2.5 billion DM) have been quickly surpassed and have recently been evaluated at 10 billion DM.

Although various experts believe that the problems of the building programs of the universities are due mainly to a difficult situation in the building market and the opposition of professors to the centralization of common administrative services, it seems that the difficulties stem more from a profound difference of opinion among planners, economists, educators, and public authorities as to the future increase in the number of students. Indeed, some policymakers are very skeptical about the expected continuous increase in the number of students (as was the case in the 1950's) and are thus reluctant to invest large sums in buildings.

Problems and differences of opinion with regard to forecasting the number of students applying for entrance into the university. During the 1950's there was a sharp increase in the number of students attending the University as a result of the important increase of the annual birth rate in the 1930's and in the first years of the war, bringing about, as we have seen, an overcrowding of buildings, giving rise to a serious crisis in the student/professor ratio, and provoking discussion as to whether the Abitur should any longer be a sufficient condition for entrance into the university, or whether a special entrance examination should not be introduced. We have seen that the Wissenschaftsrat rejected the introduction of a numerus clausus; however, it is interesting that, in a study on the overcrowding of universities (Uberfullung der Hochschulen) prepared for the Federal Ministry of the Interior by Dr. Scheidermann in 1959, the *temporary* introduction of a numerus clausus was suggested.

From 1943 onwards, however, the birth rate fell sharply, and consequently German authorities have not had to face the coming of a "vague demographique" during the '60s which created serious problems in other European countries during this decade. Furthermore it also seems that the increasing social demand which characterized the development of education in the late '40s and '50s in other European countries is not present in Germany. Indeed, the number of students graduating from secondary school (Abiturenten) as a percentage of an age group tends toward stabilization as we noted previously (about 8 percent of the age group). This is surprising considering the economic expansion and the rise of the standard of living in Germany, which in other European countries is considered mainly responsible for development of education at all levels, and particularly for the development of the secondary school and university. Why? Although it would be hazardous indeed to put forward reasons for this social stability, one should point out that in Germany education has never been considered, as much as in other countries, as a road toward social advancement. Moreover, university studies tend to be very long and the memory of unemployment of highly qualified professionals is still very much alive among the Germans.

Consequently, there is much discussion among German planners about the future increase in the number of students. Many argue that, as a result of the postwar decrease in the annual birth rate, the number of students will be less important in the years to come, whereas others, among whom one should mention Prof. Friedrich Edding, hold that, on the contrary, the number of students applying for entrance will increase and sufficient space and teachers should be available to respond to this increase.

The Wissenscaftsrat's report, partly reflecting this difference of opinion with regard to future student enrollment, offers three alternative projections. The lowest projections presuppose that the percentages of an age group entering the Gymnasium and obtaining the Abitur remain the same as in 1962. The highest assumes an increase in both these proportions. Differences do exist in these proportions according to the Länder and, as we pointed out, it is accepted that the "pool of ability" is not exhausted yet. But, as is mentioned in the Robbins' Report: "Current trends over the country as a whole lead the Council to conclude that it cannot be excluded that future developments will simply follow case A (the lowest projection) or even . . . fall below it." (See Table 3-5.)

Table 3-5

Federal Republic of Germany: Students in Universities and Equivalent Institutions for Selected Years[a]

Year	Lowest Projection	Highest Projection
1963/64	221,000	222,000
1967/68	203,000	212,000
1971/72	198,000	224,000
1975/76	204,000	265,000
1979/80	219,000	350,000

[a]Source: Wissenschaftsrat: Abiturienten und Studenten: Entwicklung und Vorschatzung der Zahlen 1950 bis 1980. (1964) as mentioned in: Robbins' Report, Appendix V, p. 87.

Considering the long delays in providing costly school buildings and for the training of qualified teaching personnel, problems arise for planners confronted with a choice among such differing projections.

Those policymakers advocating immediate and important investments base their forecasting on the expected increase in the Gross National Product, the attraction to the newly created universities of individuals coming from rural areas, the measures bringing about democratization of secondary and higher education, and the specific needs of the economy.

GNP and expansion of education. It is assumed that a correlation exists between the rate of expansion of education and the increase in the GNP, an assumption which is based on the experience of other countries (the most often cited example is the United States) and on the past tendencies in the German Federal Republic where the rate of admission by age group has increased on the whole at least as rapidly as the GNP per capita. In spite of the difficulties that accompany any forecast of the GNP, one estimates that the annual increase of growth for the next twenty years ("a honeymoon period for the Common Market countries" says Prof. Edding) will be about 4 percent and, consequently, the number of students applying for entrance into the university should increase at least at that rate. Accepting this forecast of an annual increase of GNP of 4 percent, the forecast of the rate of admission by Prof. Edding, presented at line number five (see Table 3-6) appears to be plausible; in fact, much more plausible than the hypothesis of a stable or decreasing rate.[11] The calculations presuppose that no institutional changes will affect the rate of admission, that is, that one will neither favor the rate of admission nor limit it through the institution of a numerus clausus.

Creation of universities and expansion of education. Since, according to the first hypothesis, the number of students will increase in the years to come, it will be necessary to create universities and to modernize the old ones. The very creation of a university, presumably in an area where no institution of higher learning existed before, will attract students who would not have otherwise considered attending a university. As in other countries, individuals abandon the idea of pursuing higher studies because of the distance between their homes and the institution. Expenditure for study increases considerably when it is not possible to live with one's family.

Democratization and expansion of education. Supporters of an increase in investment also point out that today only about 6 percent of working class children attend the university, but that trends indicate that this percentage will rise in the years to come. But, as we have seen the previous chapter, the reforms presently being introduced or studied are largely inspired by tradition and currently are limited to the possibility of transferring from one program to another in the secondary school. However, a process of democratization has started, and from a twenty-year perspective these social movements should be taken into consideration by planners.

Economy and expansion of education. The planning commissions note that the demand for admission into the university is partly motivated by the perspectives of well-paid jobs that are offered to university graduates. However, at this stage, one does not have full information on the future of these possibilities, and

Table 3-6

Population of Age 18 to 25 and Forecast of the Number of Students of University Level (1960-1970-1980 German students only)

	1960	1970 estimated figure	1980 estimated figure
1. Population of 18 to 25 years of age (in thousands)	7,200	6,500	7,200
2. Percentage of students of age 18 to 25(r) in comparison with total population	2.8	2.8	2.8
3. Number of students if r=2.8 (in thousands)	200	180	200
4. National per capita income, expressed in prices of 1960; 1960 = 100	100	150	200
5. r proportional increase in line 4	2.8	4.2	5.6
6. Number of students on the basis of r, line 5 (in thousands)	200	270	400
7. r increasing more rapidly than the foreseen increase of per capita income (100 - 175 - 250)	2.8%	4.9%	7.0%
8. Number of students according to r in line 7 (in thousands)	200	350	500

[a]Friedrich Edding, in *Aspects economiques de l'enseignement superieur*, Paris, OCDE, March 1964, p. 175.

Table 3-7

Federal Republic of Germany: Public
Expenditure for Higher Education
(1950-60)

	1950	1952	1954	1956	1958	1960
			In Current Price			
Total of public expenditure for higher education (excepting clinical education) (Millions DM)	204.0	292.0	381.5	488.0	705.1	939.3
Expenditure for staff:						
Millions DM	106.9	158.2	193.3	248.4	309.4	384.7
Percentage	52.4	54.2	50.7	50.9	43.9	41.0
Other current expenditure:						
Millions DM	49.6	59.5	83.2	105.3	215.6	279.9
Percentage	24.3	20.4	21.8	21.6	30.5	29.8
Investments:						
Millions DM	47.5	74.3	105.0	134.3	180.1	274.7
Percentage	23.3	25.4	27.5	27.5	25.6	29.2
			At the price of 1950			
Investments:						
Millions DM	47.5	60.4	87.ɔ	103.3	130.5	175.0
Percentage	23.3	23.4	25.5	24.8	22.8	24.5
Global current expenditure:						
Millions DM	156.5	197.9	256.0	313.0	441.2	540.3
Percentage	76.7	76.6	74.5	75.2	77.2	75.5
Total expenditure	204.0	258.3	343.5	416.3	571.6	715.3
Indexed on:						
index of construction price	100	123	120	130	138	157
index of cost of living	100	110	108	113	119	123

Table 3-8

Federal Republic of Germany: Gross
National Product and Public Expenditure for Education (1950-60)

	1950	1952	1954	1956	1958	1960
1. Gross national product (Billion DM)	92.7	135.6	156.4	196.4	228.5	276.6
2. Expenditure for Higher Education (excluding clinical Education) (Millions DM)	204.0	292.0	381.5	488.0	705.1	939.3
3. Net expenditure for clinical education (Millions DM)	74.5	97.6	120.5	162.1	183.5	237.9
4. Total expenditure for Higher Education (2+3) (Millions DM)	278.5	389.6	502.0	650.1	888.6	1,177.2
5. Expenditure for all other levels of education (Millions DM)	2,138.7	3,074.8	3,983.5	4,961.3	5,952.3	7,140.8
6. Total expenditure for Education (4+5) (Millions DM)	2,417.2	3,464.4	4,485.5	5,611.4	6,840.9	8,318.0
7. Line 6: percentage of line 1	2.49	2.55	2.87	2.86	2.99	3.01
8. Line 5: percentage of line 1	2.20	2.26	2.55	2.53	2.60	2.58
9. Line 4: percentage of line 1	0.29	0.29	0.32	0.33	0.39	0.43

professional orientation is still based upon the present situation in the manpower market.

However, efforts toward a better knowledge of future manpower needs have started. In particular, the Wissenschaftsrat, in cooperation with the German Research Council (Forschungsgemeinschaft) and the Federal Manpower Bureau (Bundesantalt fur Arbeitsvermittlung) has elaborated a study on the demand for medical doctors up to 1975, showing the need to stimulate students to choose this profession when entering the university, a conclusion contrary to the one reached by the German medical association, which publicly warned that many medical graduates would not be able to make a living. The Council has expressed its desire to pursue similar studies for other professions. However, it is not convinced that these manpower forecasts will solve the problem posed by planning for space that should be available in the various branches of higher education. Nevertheless, these studies are of the greatest importance (although generally not considered a strong enough basis upon which to make decisions) and efforts will be made to synchronize the number of graduates of the various faculties and branches of studies with the demands of the manpower market.

Here again conflicting opinions arise within the Council, based on varying degrees of opposition to planning education in terms of manpower needs. "Less credit is attached to the utility of provisions concerning the plain increase or decrease of 'employment possibilities,' particularly because these studies only reach several possibilities of choice. The elaboration of these variables presupposes a training which one rarely finds even among the members of the organizations in charge of planning."[12]

In any case, it is clearly stated that if studies were undertaken with regard to the future situation of the manpower market, this knowledge should never lead to authoritarian orientation of the students, and should only be used to inform students which, in most cases, will be a form of orientation.

Conclusion. Apart from the administrative, technical, financial, and other problems with which one is confronted when planning, it appears from the foregoing that the main problem with regard to planning in Germany is the forecasting of the quantitative development of higher education, which, so it seems, stems from a profound difference of opinion among planners. Germany does not offer, as is the case in other European countries, an example in the recent past of an expansion of higher education mainly due to a postwar "social demand." But will this trend continue? Some believe it will not and expect that the increase in GNP per capita will necessarily stimulate the "social demand" for further education. However, apart from the technical reasons put forward to sustain the "expansionist" opinion, this difference of opinion seems to reveal much more a difference of opinion concerning the educational and social policy to be adopted. We have noted before that the efforts toward a reorganization of the secondary school have been concentrated on the possibility of passage between the parallel types of education through the creation of "Aufbau Form" classes in the "Realschulen" and gymnasiums; consequently they do not deal with the structural reform of secondary education. Other projects of reform have been elaborated but have been rejected either by the teaching personnel or by the public. This applies in particular to the "Plan For a New Organization," known also as the "Bremer Plan," whose efforts for democratization of education on the basis of socialist principles have been considered incompatible with German cultural traditions, which are based upon the conception of a "literary and classical" secondary school reserved to the traditional elite which formed the governing classes of the past. German education – a "liberal" education with delay?, wonders Rev. Mario Reguzzoni.[13]

Thus, it is not at all certain that the "expansionist" theory will prove right, in spite of an expected increase of GNP, and perhaps "social stability" with regard to education is not due to disinterest on the part of the public but on the incapacity of education to attract, in its present form, new social classes. In Germany the needs of the economy, which elsewhere have stimulated the reforms, might not be a stimulating factor because of the unquestionably high level of technical and professional training available in German technical educational institutions.

France

Considered rightfully one of the free enterprise countries in which economic and educational planning is the most developed, France's answer to the International Bureau of Education inquiry is ambiguous and very surprising to outsiders. It states that:

there is no specially organized educational planning in France (but) it is to be noted however that a commission for school, university, and sports equipment (the Le Gorgeu Commission) was set up to consider projections for the development of national education until 1970 and to study in particular not only the human and material means which must be found but also the educational and administrative reforms for which provision should be made.[14]

This reserve and deliberate ambiguity on the part of the Ministry of National Education stems partly from the fact that the educational development plan is part of the general perspectives of the national plan; but it stems also from the liberal tradition in which one would never admit, de facto or de jure, that the state, through its development plans, can impose a specific type of education, excluding or neglecting other types. This same prudence is found in the other Western European countries.

Nevertheless, France, since 1946, stimulated its economic development through a rational organization of its economy with the help of national plans determining the volume and orientation of public and private investments, accompanied by studies on the corresponding evolution of manpower needs and the means to satisfy these needs. At first, the "Commissariat General du Plan" limited its studies to the six basic industrial sectors which were given priority because of the losses they suffered during the Second World War. But from 1951 onwards the preliminary studies for the Second Plan (1953-57) considered the whole of the country's activities. The whole of private and public investments and the social and administrative sector were included in the framework of economic growth targets. Consequently, alongside the commissions concerned with economic modernization, commissions dealing with social problems (housing, school, sanitation, equipment) were set up.

Created in 1951, the Commission de l'Equipment Scolaire et Universitaire, launched the first studies aimed at a rational and systematic analysis of the future development of education as a whole.

In answer to the question of why these problems of the development of education have their place within the work of the Commissariat of the Plan, Raymond Poignant points out at some length:

In the beginning the reason was very simple: State education is one of the most important public services and one of the costliest; it is therefore essential for the economists of the Plan, in their study of fixed capital formation and consumption by government services, to take into account the changing needs for education services. It was primarily for this purpose that the Commission was first set up in 1951 and this was the chief consideration underlying its first report ... But the work of the Commission soon brought to light another important consideration: the work of the Commissariat du Plan being to determine the volume of investment in the various sectors and the volume and distribution of manpower, there naturally tends to be a direct relationship between the demand for skilled or highly qualified manpower revealed by the Plan and the problems of educating the country's youth; it is increasingly evident that investment in education, especially technical, vocational, and higher education, must be guided by the foreseeable development of employment.

Seen in this light, the development of education becomes a dynamic factor acting directly on economic growth; expenditure on schools and universities is no longer seen as administrative expenditure but as intellectual investment," the level of which can determine in the long run the rate of economic development ... It is on the basis of these two considerations that the Commission is continuing its work.[15]

Mission, composition, and working methods of the Commission. The following discussion will deal with the Commission in terms of its mission, composition, and working methods, and their relationship.

1. Mission. The Commission's mission is fourfold: (1) It evaluates the global volume of public investment (building and equipment needed during the years covering the Plan to satisfy the needs of the various levels of education, and the distribution of the financing of that investment between the state and local authorities – departments and communes); (2) It estimates the needs for teachers corresponding to the increase in the number of students, and formulates measures needed to recruit the teaching staff; (3) As a secondary activity the Committee also determines the geographical allocation of education investments in cooperation with the "Regional Plans Committee," in an effort to remodel the economic regions of France through judicious allocation of investment.

However, this concerns only institutions of higher learning (including higher technical education). For the other levels of education, the Commission determines only the overall volume of investment needed according to the trend of school attendance, while the location of schools is decided by the Ministry of Education in cooperation with the Regional Educational Committees (Commission academiques) and the National Commission of the School Map (Commission Nationale de la Carte Scolaire), and (4) It studies administrative and technical measures which should be followed to expedite investment in education.

The Commission's mission concerns only public education (the Ministry of Education does not finance investment in private education) which is controlled by the Ministry of Education (95 percent of public investment in education) and does not concern certain categories of vocational education, especially agricultural education which is controlled by the Ministry of Agriculture and whose needs are studied by the Agricultural Committee of the Plan. Although cooperation between the Education and Agricultural Committees exists, French education planners do not seem to be satisfied with this organization and recommend that all matters concerning education be considered jointly.

2. Composition. The Education Commission has the same general structure as the other commissions of the Commissariat du Plan. It is composed of representatives of the public authorities concerned: *Ministry of Education:* Strongly represented on the Commission and also on the working parties. The Commission's Report is thus the fruit of cooperation between the Ministry of Education on the one hand and, on the other hand, the Plan officials, other Ministries, and representatives of trade unions and employer's federations with the heads of all the Departments of the Ministry; and one rector, two deans, one principal of a college of technology (Directeur d'Ecole d'Ingenieurs). *Ministry of Finance:* Budget, Treasury, Economic and Financial Surveys Departments. *Ministry of the Interior, Ministry of Construction:* "amenagement du territoire" Department, responsible for regional development. *Municipalities:* represented by three mayors. *Employers' Representatives:* two members, including the chairman of the Vocational Training Committee of the C.N.P.F., the French Employers' Federation. *Trade union and teaching staff representatives:* four members. *Representatives of the Conseil Economique:* two members, both chosen from among the representatives of "Associations familiales." *Other members:* appointed in a personal capacity from the public or private sectors, including in particular the chairman of the Manpower Committee of the Commissariat du Plan. In all the Committee consists of about forty members.

3. Working methods. The Commission primarily employs two methods. The first method is to make inquiries among regional education administrators (rectors, deans, academy inspectors, etc.) carried out by the Ministry of Education; these inquiries provide for each category of education an inventory of the equipment required in each district in terms of demographic, economic, and social trends, and the replacement needs for existing schools. These inventories are prepared in cooperation with the local official in charge of regional planning and indicate precisely the location of each item of educational investment requested. Processed and summarized by Ministry of Education officials, they provide a first source of information on school population trends, needs for the replacement of old and unsuitable premises, needs resulting from population shifts, and location of future establishments. The second method is to conduct surveys on a national level by working parties of the Commission: they consist in forecasting the trend of the total student population at the various education levels in the light of demographic, social, and economic factors assessed at the national level. The resultant synthesis is compared with the findings of the inquiries among education authorities.[16]

Forecasting educational development in terms of demographic, social, administrative, and economic factors. Development of France's educational system has been extraordinary over the last fifteen years. Forecasting this development at the different levels of education is a complex venture in which various factors have to be taken into account.

1. Demography. France's population boom started from 1946 onwards (840,000 annual births against 612,000 in 1939), replacing successively at all levels of education smaller age groups of prewar period. The "vague demographique" reached nursery schools in 1949, primary schools in 1952, secondary schools in 1957 and the university in 1964. At this rate, it is expected that annual births will rise to 922,000 in 1975. As long as the compulsory school age is taken as a guide, the effects of demography on equipment and teachers are rather easy to evaluate. However, difficulties arise even at this level because in certain regions the number of school-going children may increase or decrease because of population shift (urbanization, large new housing projects) and also because the birth rate may differ from the national average.

2. Social factors. Expansion of secondary and higher education is also a consequence of social demand. Here forecasting of student enrollment becomes more delicate. But an analysis of the rate of expansion of these types of education from 1950 onwards permits fairly accurate extrapolation with regard to the continuous trend of social demand. However, one must take into consideration when elaborating these forecasts, the differences which appear in the social and geographic origin of the child.

Traditionally, French education systems are free, and access to secondary and higher education is free to all citizens. It is on the basis of this liberalism that the Planning Commission proceeds.

3. Administrative factors: The evolution of student enrollment is closely dependent on government measures, and government measures in France, as elsewhere in Europe, tend towards expansion of education rather than to limitation. In France, with regard to governmental measures, the Planning

Commission takes into consideration the extension of compulsory school age attendance rising to 16 years of age from 1972 onwards, and the organization of education. The reforms introduced at the secondary school level in 1959 are expected to increase the number of students enrolling in the university.

To expedite the extension of compulsory studies the reform implies the grouping together (in most cases by 'busing') of all the children of a particular region after completion of primary school (five years of study), and makes increased capital expenditures necessary. The planning Commission has no prerogatives with regard to the reforms, and must limit itself to the application of these reforms.

4. Economic factors. Adopting the theory that a reciprocal link exists between economic growth and the development of education, the French Planning Commission emphasizes the continuous shift of the active population from the primary sector (rapid decrease in the total volume of employment) to the secondary sector (slow increase tending to stabilization) and the tertiary sector (rapid increase) with increasing demands in the three sectors for higher qualification of the labor force.

The problem with which the Planning Commission deals, then, is the most desirable distribution of the number of students, which it previously calculated, among the various types of learning corresponding to the nation's activities; thus among the various types of secondary schools (technical, professional, general), and the various types of higher education (letters and human sciences, sciences, law, medicine, engineering, etc.). It is in terms of this distribution of the total number of students among these various types of education that the Commission will decide the volume of investment to be made and dedicated to each type of school.

However, to solve this problem of distribution, one needs to know what the future needs in manpower will be for the various professional activities, and what qualifications are necessary.

At this stage, the Commission for Education must rely on the studies and predictions of the manpower Committee (Commision de la Main-d'Oeuvre) presided over by Mr. Fourastie, Director at the Ecole Pratique des Hautes Etudes (Sorbonne).

Mr. Fourastie's Commission has as its task the forecasting of the evolution in number and qualifications of the individuals active in the various professional branches during the duration of the Plan, that is, four or five years. These forecasts are of great interest for other planning commissions, but they are too short term to enable the Commission for Education to proceed to its forecasting, since it takes a long time to train an individual. At best, the investments made in education relate to the economic plan of eight to ten years ahead. The distribution of the approximately 500,000 students who will be attending the university in 1970 can be made only when one takes into consideration the probable structure in number and qualification of the labor force of 1975.

Consequently, the Commission for Education asked the manpower Commission to pursue its studies and predictions up to 1975.

From the point of view of general economic planning, the Manpower Commission asks the national education system to provide men capable of making the national economy work. The problem, then, for industry and the whole of the French economy, is to have available men sufficiently educated, capable of using modern techniques in the most effective way for the economy. What is required is not only qualified personnel, but personnel qualified in rather precise, numerous, and varied techniques.

Mr. Fourastie points out the difficulties:

It is not only difficult to say with confidence, (We need in 1975, I suppose, 12,500 engineers specialized in metallurgy at this particular level of qualification . .) but it is even more difficult to foresee what these engineers will have to know, the methods they will have to apply in metallurgy in 1975; to foresee these methods is even inherently foreign to the notion of progress, for if we already knew these methods of 1975, we would be applying them: consequently we do not know the precise techniques which will be used by these engineers.

Consequently neither the Manpower Commission, nor the Education Commission can foresee what precisely students ought to know, although they are currently in school. This is one of the dramas of the present situation; we have to train youngsters for a world which we do not know and about which we have only vague ideas despite our best forecasting efforts.

I cannot insist enough on this . . . we have to train our children much more for an intellectual flexibility than for the knowledge of certain known techniques. We have to give them above anything else the aptitude to educate themselves to the techniques which they will be applying in 1975. Our problem is not to teach them what they will have to know in 1975; our problem is to teach them what is necessary for them to know today so that, little by little, they can learn themselves by 1975 what they will have to know at that moment.[17]

And Mr. Fourastie concludes that, consequently, one must attempt to foresee the number of students not in terms of programs of study but in terms of "directions of culture."

Forecasting the labor force. Labor force forecasting is conducted in two stages. In the first stage, prediction is in terms of the various branches of activity. It consists of forecasting the labor force by branch of activity, that is, one will have to foresee the number of individuals active in agriculture, metallurgy, textile, automobile industry, etc. The reason for this first forecasting is that the qualifications of individuals are quite different in each branch of activity. A prediction of qualifications made on the basis of the total French active population would not be possible, or at least it would be very inaccurate.

At the second stage, one forecasts the skills of the individuals in each branch, skills which are graded according to six levels, establishing relations between the education received and the future profession. These correlations have no value as rules except for professions with a legal statute (e.g., medicine, law), but they can give an idea of the average situation (see Table 3-9).

Table 3-9

Average Relationships between Employment and Education

Level	Employment	Education (Humanities and Science)	No. of years of Education after the end of the "Cycle d'Observation"
1	Highly responsible and complex management functions, heads of departments, technologists and teachers requiring very thorough knowledge of vast and difficult fields	At least one year after the "licence d'enseignement complete"	At least 10
2	Functions requiring a sound knowledge of difficult fields	University degree or diploma in technology	At least 9
3	Technicians and administrators performing functions requiring good knowledge in relatively limited fields	Two years, or at least one year after baccalaureat or diplome de technicien	6, or more generally 7
4	Supervisors (foremen) and assimilated	Baccalaureat or diplome de technicien level	On average 5
5	Skilled workers (manual and clerical)	"Certificat professionnel" level	3 to 4
6	Unskilled workers	- - - -	1 year (or 3 years when school-leaving age is raised to 16)

Remarks: To illustrate this chart one could point out that agriculture, for example, does not require more than 0.5 percent of its labor force to possess university training, whereas in education the proportion of individuals possessing university degrees is about 30 percent. In general, the primary sector demands less trained personnel than the secondary and tertiary sectors.

Proceeding with the plan. When the plan has been elaborated according to the methods we outlined above, and the necessary investments have been calculated, the next question is: how will one proceed to the implementation of the Plan?

There will be arbitration between the demands for investment funds formulated by the various commissions. The commission for education has now, with other commissions, presented its demands for investment. However, the investments which can be made during the period of the plan are necessarily limited, particularly the public investments (housing, roads, hospitals, schools, etc.) and the demands for investment tend to exceed considerably the possibilities of financing. Consequently, it is necessary to proceed to an arbitration among the various demands so as to limit the investments to the possibilities of finance.

This arbitration is conducted by the General Commissariat of the Plan, in close cooperation with the Commissions concerned and the Ministries. In case of a persistent disagreement between these three government bodies (Commission, Commissariat, and Ministries), the question is decided by the Prime Minister at a cabinet meeting.

The battle of priorities. It is at this high level of decision-making that the general public is informed of the options of the Plan, and battles for priorities start between the various commissions and the professions directly affected by the government's decisions. For example, the Education Commission holds the government responsible for the delays in execution of the plan and the resulting problems for education (shortage of buildings, lack of qualified professionals). The Commission pointed out on the occasion of the Second Plan that only 65 percent of its demand for investment had been satisfied, and only 80 percent for the Third Plan. At this level, the question of priorities can become highly political; for example, the government's decisions concerning the Fifth Plan and the reactions to it.

In July, 1965, after the government's decisions, it was clear that education would not receive the "super priority" that observers expected, and Le Monde reports that a "public opinion poll" not made public by the government showed that the public was more interested in getting the right roads (good highways are terribly lacking in France) and telephones (it is usual to wait for six months or more in Paris to obtain a telephone line). One should not forget that 1965 was a presidential election year in France. The government decided to propose to Parliament the low forecast, i.e., 25 billion francs (over the five year plan period) for education, which represents a 20 percent increase compared with the finances made available for the previous plan; considering that the earlier plan covered only four years and considering also the increase in general level of prices, the increase is weaker than the one registered for the Fourth Plan.

The Commission had first demanded 32 billion francs, stating that this amount corresponded to the satisfaction of needs and was indispensable considering the reforms introduced and the demographic, economic, and social evolution. With 25 billion francs the government would have to radically change its education policies: notably it would have to delay for another two years the organization of a complete first cyclus. The reforms of 1959 had provided that the minimum school-leaving age would be extended to age sixteen from 1967 on. However, the Government later decided that this new measure would be applied from 1972 on, when all the material required to receive all the children from age eleven on would be available. The Education Commission stated that with the 25 billion francs, this 1972 goal would not be attained either. "The prolongation itself of this delay would be unacceptable. 230,000 children could not possibly be received in the first cyclus. Despite the fact that the Fifth Plan had to be for education the realization of a fundamental goal: a lower secondary school open to all children."[18]

When the different investments have finally been decided, the Commissariat du Plan constructs a general report which is submitted to Parliament for discussion. The figures indicated in this document are for guidance only and do not commit the Ministry of Finance. "In fact, they constitute the guiding pattern of public investment as finally decided — either when the annual budget is voted; or when special programs are voted by Parliament."[19]

Adapting the execution of the Plan to economic needs. Apart from the financial question and the difficulties related to it, a number of administrative and technical problems must be dealt with before the educational development plan can be carried out. One of these problems is of great concern; it is the adaptation of the execution of the Plan to economic needs.

Apart from the problem of distributing the investment at the different levels of education and the fixing of the most suitable location of the establishments "which are most important from the economic standpoint: technical colleges, higher institutions, and higher technical establishments,"[20] there remains the problem of "determination of the educational syllabi" (i.e., the organization of the specialized subjects taught in the school) and of the orientation of students.

Determination of educational syllabi. The forecast of the volume of investment has been calculated on the basis of the overall enrollment objectives by major categories of schools (general, vocational, technical), taking into account as far as possible the long-term trends in the active population. However, with the implementation of the Plan and with the construction of new schools or the extension of old ones, a more precise inquiry must be undertaken by the Ministry of Education in cooperation with trade associations (Comites departementaux de l'Enseignement technique, the Commissions Nationales professionnelles de l'Enseignement technique, the Commission nationale interprofessionnelle) for technical and vocational institutions, so as to elaborate the exact curriculum of the subjects and courses to be taught. "For example," says Raymond Poignant, "it is, at this stage, no longer sufficient to have a total figure for industrial apprentices: the total figure calculated by the Committee must now be apportioned among the various industrial sectors (electricians, plumbers, fitters, etc.) and similarly the number of candidates for the various types of training in institutes of technology must be calculated."[21] As regards the technical lycees and colleges, the teaching programs of new or expanded establishments must allow for manpower needs as they appear either at local or at national level (e.g., regions with emigrating labor). For this purpose, the educational authorities work in close cooperation with the Manpower Commission, which gives a fairly good picture on a short-term basis of the number of skilled workers required in each sector. With regard to this, there is a continuous development and a series of limited decisions taken throughout the period covering the Plan.

Orientation of students. There is nothing compulsory in the 'distribution' of young people by the Commission in the light of estimated trends in the active population. Experience shows that the establishment of new schools and adequate information given to families are sufficient to insure that young people will be channeled in a direction consistent with employment trends.[22]

In the vocational, technical, and higher technological schools, the teaching programs are laid down by the authorities, and consequently the "channeling" of the students in directions consistent with the tendencies on the manpower market can be achieved satisfactorily. But this "channeling" is much more difficult to do at the university level where, within each faculty, the student is free to choose his speciality (for example, in the Faculty of Science, he could choose between chemistry, physics, biology, geology, etc.), although the Plan's expansion policies for the various faculties might contribute to the orientation of the student toward a faculty, they do not have such an effect. Planners insist on the necessity for a more effective orientation of the students in terms of the structural trends of the active population. Raymond Poignant points out that the number of geology and natural science students seems to be in excess of requirements. There is no limititation on the number of students in the various specialized branches.

The development of higher education in France up to 1970 and the new educational plan 1966-1970. The new educational plan of the Fifth French Plan covers five years (the Fourth Plan covered four years), from 1966 to 1970. In 1970 the reforms applied from 1959 onwards and concerning mainly the secondary level of education, and those of 1966 dealing primarily with higher education, will have been completed and produced their effects. By that same year, the population boom will have had its effects up to the highest levels of education. Consequently, 1970 is for French education something of a turning point. However, this turning point will be really reached only in 1972, as the Fifth Plan delays until 1972 the coming into effect of the provision of the 1959 reforms which had provided for an extension of compulsory school age attendance up to the age of sixteen.

To predict the attitude of the parents and students toward the new arrangements is difficult. Nevertheless, according to the Fifth Plan with respect to secondary education, 35 percent of the pupils will be oriented toward the "long" section of secondary education leading toward the "baccalaureat" or "brevet de technicien" after completion of four years of secondary studies. But 40 percent, upon completion of the same first cyclus of four years, will be oriented toward the "short" secondary cyclus, or towards active life. These are the desired percentages. Will it be so? It is difficult to foresee the percentages of failures and of pupils who abandon their studies. However, on all these points, it seems that the Commission, as for the Fourth Plan, has been led to make strong assumptions on the needs of the French economy for highly skilled and medium skilled personnel. At the same time, the Commission notes that these needs might not be satisfied, despite the tremendous increase in the number of students (which will have more than doubled in eight years). Therefore, any malthusianism must be dismissed, for social reasons, but also for economic reasons.

These needs might not be satisfied because of a bad distribution of the number of students among the various disciplines. The Fourth Plan had estimated that 42 percent of the students should be oriented toward scientific disciplines, and had foreseen that this percentage would be reached in 1969. Will it be reached in 1972, as the Commission which prepared the Fifth Plan hopes? It is doubtful considering that, contrary to the predictions, the proportion of secondary school graduates choosing the section "mathematiques ele- mentaires" – preparing secondary school students toward the scientific disciplines – has decreased over the last few years to reach the figure of 24 percent, the same as in 1954. The reason? "The program of study of this section is too ambitious," and the Commission states: "The sections (of the secondary degree) predominantly mathematical must be opened to all the students capable of following the teaching. The solution which consists of reserving these sections to the particularly brilliant elements whom one believes to have the vocation to enter later classes preparing for the 'grandes ecoles,' must be condemned."

The Fifth Plan's forecast of the number of students entering the second cyclus of secondary school (35 percent of an age group) and higher education (20 percent) is the result of an overall policy adopted by the government which the Commission took into consideration. These percentages, although they are higher for example than in West Germany and Great Britain, risk, however, not meeting the demands of families, the "social demand." Le Monde notes: "They will only be controlled through a more strict selection than is presently the case, and probably through a selection procedure upon entrance into higher education."

The essential task of the Commission was then to calculate the cost in new equipment made necessary by this policy. It first presented a number of cost estimates based on a series of forecasts. The most generous hypothesis, which was based upon a decrease in the student/professor ratio (particularly in primary and secondary education), needed an investment of 35 billion FF. The lowest hypothesis of the Commission demanded an investment of 26.7 billion FF. The figure finally adopted by the government is 25.5 billion FF, of which 20.5 billion is financed by the state and 5 billion by the local communities.

A comparison of these appropriations with those made under previous plans shows the following progression (variations in cost can be regarded as negligible between 1952 and 1961):

1948-1952 (5 years):	FF	2,000 million
1953-1957 (5 years):	FF	6,000 million
1958-1961 (4 years):	FF	8,200 million
1962-1965 (4 years):	FF	11,500 million

Remarks. The sums appropriated during the first years of the Fourth Plan were made with a currency whose purchasing power was higher. Taking into consideration the increase in the cost of building, the sums appropriated for the Fourth Plan, translated into francs of 1965, reach about 13,000 million. The real increase of the sums appropriated for the Fifth Plan in comparison with the previous one and over a similar period of time would be 25 percent less if the increase of prices continued to be strong.

Yet, France dedicates greater sums to educational investment than many other developed countries, approximately one-third of the total sum financing collective civilian equipment (housing, roads, telephone, hospitals, etc.). In the course of the Fifth Plan this share will remain constant, since the budget of equipment for national education will progress at the average rate of civilian investments, that is 8 percent per annum. Applying this percentage, the budget of equipment for national education will be, in 1967, approximatively 3,700 million FF, compared with 3,500 million in 1966 (investments for research excluded). Although these sums remain high, observers believe that the "expansionist" policy of the government in matters of education will not find its full application.

Conclusion. Although it is impossible at the time of writing to make a full appraisal of the Fifth French Plan with regard to education, due to the lack of documents which will not be available for some time, we can give a tentative appraisal. At first it should be noted that French educational planning benefits from special circumstances, and particularly from the existence of an overall economic and social plan and a centralized system of educational structures. It should also be noted that its elaboration is not the work of a small number of "technicians" but the result of combined efforts of teachers, unions, government officials, and officials of the municipalities. "Nor is it predominantly theoretical," says Raymond Poignant, "since however important the basic studies may be, the work is essentially practical, the main difficulties being the administrative — and financial — realities of the moment."[23]

However, it should be strongly stressed that planning as presently organized proceeds without the ability to question the organization of education: the structures of education have not as yet been the subject of planning, but are a given, a framework which imposes itself on planning. Furthermore, the planning decisions seem to a very large extent an effort of adaptation to the limited possibilities offered by the budget, which are the "realities of the moment." If it were otherwise, one would deny the "very essence of planning," i.e., that the "resources sought for education are bound to be weighed against other national needs and that discriminating between these needs can be done only by the highest national authorities . . . "[24]

Belgium

The reply sent by the Ministry of Education to the International Bureau of Education inquiry indicates that there is no overall plan for the development of all aspects of education and that any decision taken with respect to educational development is based on the Act of May 29, 1959, signed by the national political parties, which provides that parents should be offered a school situated within a reasonable distance and the kind of education which they have chosen for their children.

The state has thus a two-fold task in that it must organize in all regions throughout the territory an official education which satisfies without discrimination all the needs of the population, and at the same time, subsidize the establishments which are organized by the subordinate organs of power (provinces, communes) or by private persons (in most cases ecclesiastical authorities or religious communities) provided that such establishments are run in conformity with legal requirements (sufficient enrollment, educational level, etc.).[25]

Financial measures, particularly with regard to construction of new schools, have been taken to complete the objectives of the Act.

The Ministry states:

The existence of three, often rival, education networks (organized by the state, subordinate organs, and private persons) has so far constituted the greatest obstacle to any endeavors made in planning. The idea of planning is undoubtedly gaining ground, but in practice any proposed measures are resisted by those who are in favor of one or another network and who are aware of the particular disadvantages for them which would necessarily follow any decision favoring the nation's community as a whole.[26]

This statement reflects the situation in which any proposition for reforms, planning, or financing of education at all levels, including higher education, must be formulated. The reform of secondary education and its consequent relative democratization were made possible only through the School Pact (Pacte scolaire) signed in 1958 by the three traditional political parties (Social democrat, Socialist and Liberal) bringing about the Act of May 29, 1959, and an end to the violent battles dominating educational politics for over a century.

After the declaration of independence and the ousting of Guillaume d'Orange, who wanted state monopoly in education, the Belgians adopted a Constitution (Feb. 7, 1831) granting freedom of education and submitting to the law only those institutions financed by the state. From that period onward two systems developed in Belgium; one public and neutral, directed by the Public powers (state, provinces, communes); the other "free," dominated by the Catholics.

The second major difficulty for educational development and planning stems from the bilingual character of the state (Belgium, 9,078,000 inhabitants, of which 44 percent are French-speaking, the remaining, Dutch-speaking). As one government official put it, "If in this country you decide to create a technical school, then you must immediately think that in fact that means creating four technical schools, two in the Dutch-speaking part of the country (one official, one 'free') and two in the French-speaking part of the country." Any plan or program will reflect this situation, meaning a heavy financial burden for the country and creating complex social, political, and economic problems.

It is with respect to this that one must understand the complexities of the Law on university expansion adopted on April 9, 1965, under the pressure of an ever-increasing number of students enrolling at the four universities or assimilated institutions and the needs of economic and social development.

In his expose of the motives of the government's program of university expansion to the Senate on June 25, 1964, the then Prime Minister Theo Lefevre stated that our society is coming to be characterized by less rigid social stratification.[27] Democratization and increasing the output of graduates, "a decisive effect upon our competitive chances on a long-term basis," are the chief concerns of the Belgian government.

Various new elements, according to the prime minister, should influence the increase in the number of students, among others, the effects of the reforms of the secondary school system (polyvalence); an increasing participation of female students; and the opening of new university centers in areas which have never had a university institution.

One will deal with these various expansion problems in two phases: the first one covering the period 1965-68; the second with no end date but starting with the academic year 1968.

Referring to the development, the selection problems, and the rationalization of non-university institutions (technical schools), the Minister made it clear that it would be necessary to orient a larger number of secondary school graduates toward these institutions, "better responding to the aptitudes of a great number of youngsters and the development of which is necessary for the national economy."[28]

With regard to finance, he stated that each year discussions will take place in Parliament deciding what part of the national revenue Belgium is ready to spend on higher education, how these funds must be distributed, and at what rhythm the execution of the proposed program should be carried out.

A central body is charged with the responsibility for higher education and its expansion. The "Conseil National de la Politique Scientifique" (National Council for Scientific Policy), and its subordinate group, "Expansion of Higher Education," have the mission to study and to make proposals in close liaison with the universities and the assimilated institutions of higher education; to promote the adequate development of the institutions of higher learning in terms of the needs of the country; and to expand research and increase the number of students.

The Act of April 9, 1965, containing various measures favoring expansion of higher education, stipulates in its article 72 that the National Council for Scientific Policy will constitute a special commission to study the application of the measures presented in the law. This Commission is composed of four rectors from the four universities and of personalities from the economic, social, and scientific worlds, and was to deliver a report by October 1967, with regard to the problems of higher education expansion.

Furthermore, a permanent political commission, composed of representatives of the three national parties (called the Commission of the School Pact), will be following the problems of university development and expansion.

The Scientific Council has stated its preoccupations with regard to its mission, which will give us an idea of the methods that the Council intends to pursue to bring about university expansion in Belgium, which in future will be based on the findings of the Council's studies and on its advice.

The Council estimates that the essential facts which will have to be gathered are of three kinds:

1. The following facts as they present themselves today: (a) Sociological facts — total number of students per faculty; percentage enrolled per age group of the population of the age of higher education; geographic distribution of students; social origin, social status, and housing of the students. (b) Pedagogical facts — distribution of the teaching personnel per faculty (see Table 3-10); student/professor ratio per faculty; organization of teaching per faculty; percentage of failures per faculty; percentage of postgraduates per branch of study. (c) Financial facts — relation of expenditures for higher education to the national product and the current expenditures of the state; cost of the researcher, professor, and student per faculty; cost of equipment per faculty; cost of investment per faculty; process of attribution and consumption of finances for teaching and research at the various levels. (d) Economic facts — utilization of the individuals graduating from institutions of higher learning per socioeconomic category, per branch of study and per level of qualifications; scarcity or abundance of these individuals on the employment market.

2. Following this, one would have to project the principal qualifying factors over a number of years, especially those relating to the increase of the number of students and teaching personnel; the chosen branches of studies; the increase of the expenditures for functioning, equipment, and investment in terms of the number of students and their qualifications which will be in demand by socio-economic category.

3. One should then assemble comparable facts about the evolution of this situation in those countries surrounding Belgium. On the basis of all these facts, the Council hoped to have an opinion on the main policy lines which will be

Table 3-10

Belgium: Number of Teaching, Scientific, and Associate Staff of the Institutes of Higher Education
(Academic year 1962-63)

Institution	Teaching Staff			Assoc. Staff			Scien. Staff			Total		
	FT^a	PT^b	T	FT	PT	T	FT	PT	T	FT	PT	T
University of Ghent	181	51	232	28	--	28	355	36	391	564	87	651
University of Liege	145	21	166	39	3	42	406	24	430	590	48	638
University of Brussels	173	374	547	14	--	14	221	281	502	408	655	1063
University Catholique de Louvain	287	253	540	18	--	18	138	--	138	443	253	696
Faculte polytechnique de Mons	44	9	53	--	--	--	28	--	28	72	9	81
School of Vet. Medicine at Cureghem	12	--	12	--	--	--	12	--	12	24	--	24
Agronomic Institute at Gembloux	28	14	42	--	--	--	21	--	21	49	14	63
Agronomic Institute at Ghent	28	15	43	--	--	--	28	--	28	56	15	71
St. Louis U. Faculty at Brussels	8	8	16	--	--	--	--	--	--	8	8	16
Univ. Faculty N-D de la Paix at Namur	32	32	54	--	--	--	6	5	11	38	27	65
Royal Military Academy	35	3	38	--	--	--	45	--	45	80	3	83

(continued)

Table 3-10 (*continued*)

Institution	Teaching Staff			Assoc. Staff			Scien. Staff			Total		
	FT[a]	PT[b]	T	FT	PT	T	FT	PT	T	FT	PT	T
Higher State Institute of Commerce: Antwerp	54	63	117	--	--	--	--	--	--	54	63	117
School for higher economic and Consular studies, Leige	13	62	75	--	--	--	--	--	--	13	62	75
Commercial Institute St. Ignace: Antwerp	8	24	32	--	--	--	--	--	--	8	24	32
Institute of economics and consular studies at Mons	12	39	51	--	--	--	--	--	--	12	39	51
Institute of economics, Mons	13	27	40	--	--	--	--	--	--	13	27	40
Catholic Institute of higher Economic studies, Brussels	10	44	54	--	--	--	--	--	--	10	44	54
Total	1,083	1,029	2,112	99	3	102	1,260	346	1,606	2,442	1,378	3,820

[a]FT : Fulltime
[b]PT : Part time

recommended to the government. The evaluation of the necessary means will be conceived in terms of modern efficiency and authentic economy.

Teaching and scientific personnel of institutions of higher learning in Belgium. The following statistics have been drawn up by the National Council for Scientific Policy only as an indication, since all the necessary facts could not be gathered by the Council.

Table 3-11 shows the distribution of the teaching staff per function (teaching or scientific personnel) and degree of permanence in the institution.

Because of the great number of hierarchical degrees existing in the free institutions, it is sometimes difficult to establish their equivalence with the degrees of the state institutions. Uniformity of the personnel statute is recommended by the Council so as to facilitate future studies concerning university personnel.

Table 3-12 traces the evolution of the number of teaching and scientific personnel from 1958 to 1963 in the two state universities. This evolution has not as yet been elaborated for other institutions, for lack of precise data, but the Scientific Council suggests that the evolution of personnel in these institutions has been similar to that in the state universities.

The table shows that the increase in the number of teaching and scientific personnel has been more rapid, during the period considered, than the increase in the number of students. In particular, the number of scientific personnel has almost doubled. It would be desirable for a complete analysis to examine the differential evolution, per faculty, of the ratio of students to teaching and scientific personnel, but such facts are not as yet available. Moreover, the Council states that no valuable conclusions can be formulated from these facts because of too limited documentation. Nevertheless, some remarks can be made relating to university personnel, based upon the conclusions of the report of the Council on "Revaluation of the personnel of State higher education institutions and scientific institutions" and on the basis of suggestions formulated by professors. The general conclusion seems to be that there is a scarcity of teaching personnel. A number of professors complain about how little time is left for their research as a result of the increasing importance of their teaching activities. Sufficient personnel would permit the instauration of active methods of education at the university.

Equipment, particularly space and buildings. Although the question of the optimum dimension of the institution of higher education has mostly been discussed, the Scientific Council in Belgium also poses the question of the optimum number of students attending courses, exercises, laboratories, and seminars of these institutions, and its further development of this question makes it relevant to point out that it tends to go into a new — at least for Belgium — direction, when it states, "The problem of the optimum number of students puts totally into question the present systems and methods."

The most frequent method of teaching is teaching excathedra, used for as

Table 3-11

**Belgium: Teaching and Scientific Staff
of State Universities** (evolution of their
number, 1958 to 1963)[a]

	1958	1959	1960	1961	1962	1963	1963/68
Teaching staff							
University of Ghent							
- Professors & assistants	170	175	183	196	201	218	128
- Associate professors & assistants	-	-	-	1	30	42	-
University of Liege:							
- Associate professors & assistants	-	-	-	18	28	28	-
- Professors & assistants	188	182	181	179	183	180	96
Total	358	357	364	394	442	468	131
Scientific personnel							
University of Ghent	204	216	285	338	354	391	192
University of Liege	251	254	348	387	409	430	171
Total	455	470	633	725	763	821	180
Grand Total	813	827	997	1,119	1,205	1,289	158
Number of students in the two state universities	1,835	8,093	8,282	8,387	8,859	9,640	123

[a]Source: For 1958 to 1962: budgets of the
Education Nationale for 1963: information published by the establishments for the
academic year 1962-63.

Table 3-12

**Belgium: Degrees and Doctorates —
Classes, Exercises, Laboratories, and
Seminars Attended Simultaneously by
More Than 60 Students at the Same
Premises**

Number of students	No. of classes	%	No. of exer-cises, labo-ratories, etc.	%	Total	%
60 - 99	250	42.6	28	70.0	278	44.3
100 - 149	218	37.1	11	27.5	229	36.5
150 - 199	81	13.8	-	-	81	12.9
200 - 249	36	6.1	1	2.5	37	5.9
250 - 299	-	-	-	-	-	-
300 - 349	1	0.2	-	-	1	0.2
350 - 399	-	-	-	-	-	-
400 - 449	-	-	-	-	-	-
450 - 499	1	0.2	-	-	1	0.2
500 and +	-	-	-	-	-	-
Total	587	100.0	40	100.0	627	100.0
Percentage	93.6	-	6.4	-	100.0	-

Table 3-13

Belgium: Candidatures: Courses, Exercises, Laboratories and Seminars Attended Simultaneously by More Than 60 Students in the Same Premises

Number of students	No. of classes	%	No. of exercises, laboratories, etc.	%	Total	%
60 - 99	279	34.7	44	51.8	323	36.3
100 - 149	184	22.9	28	32.9	212	23.9
150 - 199	103	12.8	11	12.9	114	12.8
200 - 249	84	10.4	1	0.2	85	9.7
250 - 299	62	7.7	-	-	62	7.0
300 - 349	35	4.4	1	0.2	36	4.1
350 - 399	28	3.5	-	-	28	3.1
400 - 499	10	1.2	-	-	10	1.1
450 - 499	10	1.2	-	-	10	1.1
500 - 549	3	0.4	-	-	3	0.3
550 - 599	3	0.4	-	-	3	0.3
600 - 699	-	-	-	-	-	-
700 - 749	1	0.1	-	-	1	0.1
750 - 799	2	0.3	-	-	2	0.2
Total	804	100.0	85	100.0	889	100.0
Percentage	90.4	-	9.6	-	100.0	-

Table 3-14

Belgium: Distribution of Direct Credits
Attributed to Higher Education
(1965 to 1968)

Objectives	% of direct credits to High. Ed.	1965 (millions of Frs)	1966 (millions of Frs)	1966 increase compared to 1965 (mill. Frs)	1967 (mill. Frs)
Teaching	63.6	2,045	2,720.6	675.6	3,210.3
Fundamental research	16.6	533	710.1	177.1	837.9
Research in liaison with industry. Subsidiary activities in liaison with industry	5.7	182	243.8	61.8	287.7
Research in liaison with agriculture. Subsidiary activities in liaison with agriculture	2.0	64	85.5	21.5	100.9
Other activities of applied research	4.6	148	196.8	48.8	232.2
Other subsidiary	7.5	241	320.8	79.8	378.6
Total	100	3,213.0	4,277.6	1,064.6	5,047.6

Objectives	1967 increase compared to 1965 (mill. F)	1968 (mill. Frs)	1968 increase compared to 1965 (mill. F)	1966-1968 total increase compared to 1965 (millions of Frs)
Teaching	1,165.3	3,783.1	1,783.1	3,579.0
Fundamental research	987.4	987.4	454.4	936.4
Research in liaison with industry. Subsidiary activities in liaison with industry	105.7	339.1	157.1	324.6
Research in liaison with agriculture. Subsidiary activities in liaison with agriculture	36.9	119.0	55.0	113.4
Other activities of applied research	84.2	273.6	125.6	258.6
Other subsidiary	137.6	446.1	205.1	422.5
Total	1,834.6	5,948.3	2,735.3	5,634.5

long as the university has existed. But this way of teaching provokes very little student participation. And in Belgium, as elsewhere in Europe, educators have expressed their preference for a way of teaching which would promote student participation. We should mention in this regard two experiences, one at the State University of Liege, the other at the State University of Ghent, where student participation has been stimulated and has greatly increased; but the experience was limited to the first two years of engineering at Liege and the full course (up to the licence) in pedagogy at Ghent. The results of these experiences have shown an increasing percentage of success at the examinations. For example, in the first year of engineering at Liege, the percentage of success at the examinations went up from 34 percent in 1962 to 52.8 percent in 1963, the year during which the experiment was started. This new way of teaching with active student participation can be done, of course, only with small groups of students, and requires a greater number of scientific and teaching personnel and also a new type of building adapted to this relatively small number of students.

Remarks. In 1,516 cases, the number of students attending courses, exercises, laboratory work, and seminars makes active methods impossible. And the problem is particularly serious at the level of the first two years (candidature). This is mainly due to the great number of students at this level of higher education and also to the fact that IHL are obliged to group the students who have to follow courses of general training common to various sections. These courses of general training can be attended without too great a difficulty by many students, but the fact remains that it is precisely at this first level of university education that better teaching is a necessity. However, it seems that governmental bodies (such as the Council) and professors believe that excathedra courses should continue to be used, in particular to present the basic necessary principles. At the first cyclus of higher education (candidature) 65.3 percent of the courses are attended by audiences of over 100 students, whereas 48.2 percent of the exercises and laboratory work are attended by over 100 students (see Table 3-13). At the second level of education, up to the license, the respective percentages are 57.4 and 30.

This problem seems to increasingly preoccupy educators and planners who advocate the necessity of finding a solution to this question which takes into account the importance of the number of years of specialization in university training.

Italy

The Italian Ministry of Education's reply to the inquiry of the International Bureau of Education states: "A partial system of educational planning is implicit in the bill dealing with the 'ten-year plan of educational development' which is now before parliament."[29]

Submitted to the Senate on September 22, 1958, passed at its sitting of De-

Table 3-15

**Belgium: Evolution of the Financing of
Higher Education** (1965 to 1968)

(in thousands of Belg. Francs)	*1965*	*1966*	*1967*	*1968*
1. State Universities (+19.7% in 1965 25% en 1966 and 18% in 1967 & 1968)	1,112,298	1,387,000	1,636,700	1,931,300
Credits articles 26 & 28	- 45,700	- 62,100	- 73,300	- 86,500
Basis for subvention of private education	1,066,598	1,324,900	1,563,400	1,844,800
2. Free University of Brussels (current expenditure) 1965: forf.:44% -469.303. Population increase: 2.2% - 23.465. 1966, 1967, 1968 : 61%	492,768	808,189	953,674	1,125,328
3. Catholic university, Louvain (current expenditure) 1965 forf.: 44%-469,303. Population increase: 15.4% - 164,256. 1966, 1967, 1968 : 91%	633,559	1,205,659	1,422,694	1,678,768
4. Other subventions provided by the law of 1960 for IHL. (18.8%)	200,520	249,081	293,919	346,822
5. Other expenditures	495,773	545,350	599,885	659,873
6. New Institutions:				
"Candidature" in sciences, Antwerp		16,000	25,000	34,000
University centers of Antwerp and Mons		16,000	36,000	56,000
St. Ignace (Catholic IHL, Antwerp)	20,266	29,147	46,902	66,412
Catholic University, Mons		9,274	18,760	33,206
Supplement Notre-Dame de la Paix, Namur		11,924	14,070	16,603
	20,266	82,345	140,732	206,221
7. Special subsidies to free universities	149,814	-	-	-
Total	3,104,998	4,277,624	5,047,604	5,948,312

cember 9, 1959, and transmitted to the Chamber of Deputies on December 19, the ten-year plan was discussed in the VIII Permanent Commission (Education and Fine Atrs), which presented, on April 19, 1961 its report with the modifications that should be brought to the text adopted by the Senate. Parliament first adopted two "extracts" from the project so as to enable the Government to deal with the most urgent problems of education, and next adopted a three-year plan limiting to 1962-1965 the period during which the state would intervene with financial measures to encourage the development and expansion of Italian education.

Although the ten-year plan mentioned in the Ministry's reply to the International investigation was never adopted, it is of interest to consider at length what its objectives were. As stated by the Italian government:

The plan of educational development is concerned mainly with increasing the funds available for schools. It involves, in the state budget, the provision of exceptionally large additional sums, amounting to 1,386 billion Lire, in order to promote and ensure school development during the ten-year period beginning with the 1959-60 financial year and ending with the 1968-1969 financial year. The bill has three chapters, the first of which deals with school buildings, the second with steps (including the granting to pupils of scholarships as well as of assistance in its widest sense) for developing certain educational institutions, while the third relates to technical and scientific equipment, to university grants and university taxation privileges as well as the provision of additional teaching staff for all categories and all levels of education.[30]

Although the plan does not deal with school organization or programs it nevertheless presupposes school reform and should consequently be considered in relation to a series of other legislative measures which supplement it and which considers, as an integrated and systematic whole, the structural reforms of the various schools and the necessary reorganization of teaching.[31] (A statement of intention on the part of the Government?)

It is said that the plan failed mainly because of the large sums which were demanded for its execution, an obstacle foreseen by the government. It appears to us, however, that the failure of the plan before the Italian Parliament reflects the confused situation which existed at the end of the last decade in education. This, in turn, expresses the political problems of the Italian society, prolonging a situation which existed at the end of World War II when the schools, closed in April, 1945, progressively reopened and presented structures fundamentally lagging in comparison with the rapid economic and social development of the country. However, trapped between the growing demands for education, its own limitations, and the confrontation of ideologies, the government had to take financial measures to satisfy immediate needs, postponing the necessary reforms.

The question was to create an education which took into consideration the real necessities of the common good, instead of the ideologies of the different parties. In particular, with regard to education for fourteen- to nineteen- year-olds, one ran against a conception profoundly rooted in Italian society, encouraged during the whole period of the fascist rule, that there are two types of education: one for the people for whom the opening to a higher culture was not considered necessary, and the other reserved for the leading classes.[32]

The government's proposed ten-year plan, however, had the great merit of transforming into a concrete proposal the various discussions in political and educational circles and the studies undertaken by various specialists in education over a period of almost fifteen years and which, during the Third Legislature (1958-1963), brought about the introduction of "scuola media" and various other minor reforms.

But, in spite of their importance and relative "revolutionary" character, the reforms introduced do not sufficiently adapt the Italian school to the economic and social context, although they do enable the Italian worker to acquire a greater professional qualification.

Consequently, a unified plan of reforms had to be elaborated. It is with this goal in mind that on July 24, 1962 the "Commissione de indagine sullo stato e sullo sviluppo della pubblica istruzione in Italia," (Investigating Committee on the Situation and Development of Education in Italy) was set up; its report was at the basis of a ministerial report and the plan for reforms and finances.

The Commission's objectives as indicated by Article 56 of the Law of July 24, 1962, are: to indicate the development of education in terms of the school-age population, and in terms of the needs of the Italian society for secondary, artistic, and higher education, and for research, needs which are related to economic and social development, but taking into account also international relations and the participation of Italy in European organizations.

Installed on October 8, 1962, the Commission presented its report on July 24, 1963. It thus completed, for the first time in the history of Italy's educational system, a comprehensive study of education on all levels. It also presented a program of reforms, relatively precise, covering a period of ten years, with the recommendation that the plan should not be limited to a quantitative expansion and development, but should also embrace the qualitative aspects of the training of youth and the type of structures which could best stimulate quantitative and qualitative development.

In Chapter 2, we presented the conclusions of the Commission. Among its various suggestions one should mention:

1. *Introduction of three levels of higher education.* At present, Italian universities prepare their students (after four or five years or more of study) towards the degree of "laurea" and "dottorato." An intermediary degree does not exist. But the present situation of the Italian economy and its future development shows, according to the Commission, the necessity for a greater articulation and differentiation of higher education so as to train technical personnel more rapidly and more efficiently for industry and productive services, and therefore the introduction of an intermediary degree ("diploma") is recommended which would have an exclusively professional character. Next in the hierarchy of degrees would be the present "laurea" — scientific and professional. Finally, the third level of higher education would be the "dottorato di ricerca" (research doctorate).

2. *Professional training of secondary school teachers.* The Commission recommended that pedagogical training be given to secondary school teachers "who live in the illusion that a culture of university level is sufficient to be a

teacher and an educator." About 280,000 teachers should be trained over the next ten years. However, the Italian university will be able to achieve at the most, for the period 1965-1975, 106,000 graduates. Consequently, and taking into consideration the 56,000 professors who will be trained in the technical institutes, there remains a deficit of 117,000 teachers. Thus the Commission suggests that extraordinary intervention by the authorities should take place to direct a greater number of students towards the faculties and the pedagogical institutes.

3. *Technical institutes.* The present five years of study for the training of intermediary professionals should be maintained, but training should be directed more towards general culture and assure a better preparation for higher education.

The reservations of two members of the Commission on fundamental questions should be noted. They concern the relationship between professional education and the economic world, a relationship which according to the members should be determined by the state schools and not according to the development of the private schools. The public school "should be considered an autonomous agent stimulating the democratic, social, and economic progress of the country and should not be considered a secondary instrument for the choices and the orientations of the economic world." Furthermore, professional education should be determined in the framework of a regional policy and, finally, the state should be present with its schools in all production sectors and even in the educational activities tending towards the qualification and reclassification of the workers, in order to avoid making the individual subordinate to the necessities of production processes and particular goals.[33] These reservations express the Communist point of view. The Italian Communists believe that the Commission's report presents a "complex of reforms" but not "a general line of reforms," not an organic program of education which would make the introduction of a new relationship between the school and society possible.[34]

The Commission presented new solutions to the old and new problems of Italian education, and it is clear that the reforms should be introduced in coordination with the economic plans. However, according to most Italian observers, the Commission's recommendations are so "radical" given the existing structures, that their adoption and implementation will take a long period of time.

On the basis of the Commission's report, the Minister of Education, Mr. Gui, presented a descriptive report of the condition of Italian education to Parliament on March 31, 1964, after having submitted the propositions of the investigating Commission to examination by the Higher Council of National Education and the National Council for Economy and Labor.[35]

The report of Minsiter Gui. This report appears to have a double goal: one is to present a clear picture of the situation of the Italian educational system at all levels, in order to be able to take the steps which would best stimulate the improvement of education. "The novelty (in the approach of the Commission) consists in having searched for the connection between the problems of education and 'the needs of the Italian society' in terms of 'economic development and social progress' and this in a just equilibrium between the cultural values inherent to the schools and the other values discovered more recently and which make of the school a fundamental element of the socio-economic life of the country."[36] The other is to offer, "not a proposition or a draft bill . . ." but "a document of opinion,"[37] containing propositions which have but an indicative character and which are assembled according to the principle titles facilitating the description of the educational system.

We will limit our considerations to those titles which directly concern higher education; in particular, admission to the university, the introduction of three levels of education; geographic distribution of the universities and institutes in terms of economic and social development of the regions, and the development of the university in terms of the needs of the country.

1. Access to the university.[38] The Commission seeks to liberalize access to higher education. If economic, local, and family problems are among the main factors which constitute obstacles for young and promising students in entering the university, they are not the only negative elements. Indeed, it is pointed out that the geographic distribution of the institutions of higher learning considerably influences university attendance. One cites as an example the difference which exists between Northern and Southern Italy: the existence of a great number of technical institutes in the North corresponds to a large number of students attending courses in economics ("gruppo economico," i.e., economics and business, maritime economics, statistical and demographic sciences, political science) whereas in the South, the great number of classical and scientific "licei" and "Instituti magistrale" (teacher training schools) corresponds to a large number of students attending the courses of the juridical group and Letters (letters, philosophy, pedagogy, geography, modern and foreign languages and literature, Western European languages, literature and institutions, Eastern European languages, literature and institutions, oriental languages and civilizations). Financial help to the students is insufficient if one wants to eliminate this disequilibrium. It is necessary to proceed to a better distribution of institutions of higher learning, which would stimulate university attendance in the right proportions. Furthermore, apart from those who have obtained the full secondary school degree ("Licei"), it is proposed that others who have shown themselves to possess the required qualities should be admitted. To assess this quality, the creation of a one-year preparation course ("anno propedeutici") is recommended, but this last proposition has not been favorably considered by the Higher Council of Public Education.

2. The introduction of three levels of higher education. This has received the approval of both the Councils to whom the Commission's suggestions were submitted, with, however, partial reservations with respect to the type of institutions which should train towards the first degree ("Diploma") of higher education.[39]

3. Geographic distribution of university institutions in terms of the anticipated economic and social development. [40] In order to be able to meet the increase of the number of students which is expected over the next ten to twelve years, the Commission suggests the creation of new university institutes, particularly in those regions where none are provided. Moreover, it recommends drastic measures for closing some of the faculties in particular regions because of the great disparities which exist between the faculties by regions. (For example, the number of students in the faculty of science per university varies from 27 to 1,087; in economics and business from 298 to 3,013, etc.). The creation of new university centers should be guided by dynamic predictions of the number of graduates of the various types of secondary education and by the social, economic, and cultural needs of the region in the sphere of influence of the university. The Commission also recommends a differentiation of university centers from the point of view of the level of education, with multiplication in various university centers of institutions for intermediary professionals and limitation to a small number of university centers preparing toward the third degree (doctorate) of higher education. The Higher Council has favorably considered the various propositions of the Commission in this domain, but recommends that they be carried out gradually and in terms of the financial capacity of the state.

The Plan Gui. On October 2, 1964, the Minister of National Education, Mr. Gui, presented to the Senate "directing lines for the multi-annual development plan for the period following July 30, 1965" ("Linee direttive del piano di sviluppo pluriennale della scuola per il periodo successivo al 30 guigno 1965"), to which draft bills must refer so as to give to Italian education its new structure.

The plan is composed of two parts: the first describes the structural reforms which are necessary and the second calculates needs and forecasts expenditures. The plan covers a period of five years (1965-1970) and it is elaborated in such a way that one can modify the plan each year for the following five years.

We will present first the principles which are the basis of the plan, and then the proposed reforms of higher education.

The principles underlying the plan can be summarized as follows: the new university must above all reflect the democratic character of the political community of Italy. This demands that each member contribute to the well-being and welfare of all the other members. Therefore, the Legislature must "take away the economic and social barriers which limit in fact the liberty and the equality of the citizens and do not permit the total development of the human being and the effective participation of all the workers in the political, economic, and social organization of the country." Consequently, one must guarantee the conditions and the tools which will enable the education of all the members of the community.

The second principle refers to the relationship between the school and society. Contrary to the situation in the past, when the school was conceived only in terms of the personal desires of the individual, today's society poses precise problems to the school and demands that the school and education assure "the highest level of human and cultural training necessary to all the members of the community . . ."

So that the school can respond to these needs, and at the same time conserve its own autonomy, it should not subordinate its expansion and development to the economic-productive dimension. The school should also be the expression of the conscious ethics of the society. Therefore, the educational structure which the plan proposes tries to realize a just equilibrium between the proper values of the school, i.e., those which are directly educative, and the values discovered more recently which show to what an extent the school is a fundamental element of the country's economy.[41]

On the basis of these principles, the Minister proposes a series of state interventions to stimulate the expansion of compulsory education so as to submit all the children to this type of education; to open the access to the other types of education on the basis of individual capacities. Thus, the plan proposes to renovate the secondary school and higher education by reorganizing the "licei," the professional schools, and technical and artistic education, and by creating new university structures so as to achieve a better training of teaching personnel and for the development of scientific research.[42]

We will limit our observations to the proposals on higher education and their financial aspects:

1. With regard to the number and geographic distribution of the universities and faculties, and in agreement with the investigating commission, the plan proposes the creation of new state universities, the realization of which should be accomplished gradually over a five year period (1965-1970).

2. To facilitate access to higher education, the plan foresees a substantial increase in material assistance to the students; in particular, it is anticipated that, by 1970, 17 percent of the total registered students will benefit from a scholarship.

3. The introduction of three levels of study, each corresponding to an academic degree, marks the recognition of the economic and cultural requirements of the country. This applies in particular to the introduction of a "diploma" (academic degree of the first level), which will be highly stressed in studies for engineers and technicians.

In connection with the introduction of the three different levels of higher education, it is necessary to proceed to a revision of the legislation governing the examination of the ability to exercise a profession and the conditions for admission to examinations for state administration which gives a lesser value to the academic title and more value to the candidate's ability.

4. The introduction of three new academic degrees brings about important structural modifications as the investigating commission rightfully pointed out.

Table 3-16

Italy: **Expenditure for University and
Research** (Scientific)

	Budget Years			
	1964-65	*1965*	*1966*	*1967*
Personnel expenditures	49,611.0	52,963.5	65,274.7	75,208.5
Assistance: Scholarships, grants and others	5,680.0	6,751.6	10,998.5	13,436.6
Construction	10,000.0	19,185.0	65,000.0	65,000.0
Scientific research, equipment and special institutions	15,356.0	15,576.6	24,771.4	27,689.2
Total	80,647.0	94,476.7	166,044.6	181,334.3

	Budget Years		
	1968	*1969*	*1970*
Personnel expenditures	88,262.4	100,699.3	108,876.1
Assistance: Scholarships, grants and others	17,021.7	20,978.4	24,153.5
Construction	65,000.0	65,000.0	65,000.0
Scientific research, equipment and special institutions	31,510.1	35,036.9	37,183.8
Total	201,794.6	221,714.6	235,213.4

Table 3-17

**Italy: Expenditure for University and
Scientific Year**

	1965-66	1966-67	Academic year 1967-68	(in millions of lire) 1968-69	1969-70	total expenditure
Personnel expenditures	63,433.6	72,638.8	85,487.6	99,361.6	106,049.8	426,971.4
Assistance: Scholarship, grants & others	10,626.0	12,857.3	16,326.8	20,488.1	23,424.8	83,723.0
Construction	65,000.0	65,000.0	65,000.0	65,000.0	65,000.0	325,000.0
Scientific research, equip-ment & special institutions	24,314.0	27,052.9	30,863.5	34,735.3	36,541.4	153,507.1
Total	163,373.6	177,549.0	197,677.9	219,016.0	231,016.0	989,201.5

Table 3-18

Italy: Expenditure for University and
Scientific Research (millions of lire)

Expenditure	Total expenditure during budget year	
	1965 to 1969	*1965 to 1970*
Teaching personnel	255,655.0	324,177.8
Non-teaching personnel	126,753.4	167,106.7
Grants	46,031.8	62,984.1
Scholarships for graduates	11,239.5	15,114.1
Other types of assistance	11,915.5	15,242.1
Construction	279,185.0	344,185.0
Equipment	113,088.5	143,627.0
Scientific research	14,584.5	19,168.0
Special institutes	6,911.2	8,973.0
Total	865,364.4	1,100,577.8

It is necessary to define the precise modifications and the new institutes which were proposed. With regard to the degree of the first level of higher education it seems preferable that the courses and their organization be attached to the faculties. However, one should not elaborate in the abstract a model for all the articulations but leave great freedom to the faculties and universities, to adopt the best suited forms.

Generally speaking, the "Scuole Superiore" (First level of higher education) should be divided into four categories: (a) "Scuole Superiore" for technical studies for different branches of industry, commerce, administration, (for preparation of industrial technologists, veterinary assistants, agrarian experts or instructors, technical teachers in lower secondary schools, etc.); (b) "Scuole Superiore" for social studies for the formation of social assistants, experts in human relations for factories, publicity agents, statistical technicians, etc.; (c) "Scuole Superiore" for practical humanist studies for the formation of librarians, archivists, interpreters, etc.; and (d) "Scuole Superiore" for formation of secondary school physical education teachers, instructors and experts in

Table 3-19

**Italy: Estimated Expenditure for
Scientific Research** (millions of lire)

			Budget Year			
Expenditure	1965	1966	1967	1968	1969	1970
Personnel	26,111.0	32,180.4	37,077.8	43,513.4	49,644.7	53,675.9
Scholarship	495.5	993.9	1,333.1	1,337.6	1,659.6	1,937.3
Equipment	2,474.0	3,907.7	4,324.5	4,904.4	5,423.9	5,680.2
Scientific research	1,250.5	2,583.5	3,083.5	3,583.5	4,083.5	4,583.5
Special institutes	512.5	589.3	2,677.8	779.5	896.4	1,030.9
Academies & libraries	431.1	599.1	682.5	770.6	869.3	1,010.0
Total	31,274.6	40,853.9	46,979.2	54,889.0	62,577.4	67,917.8

sports. Artistic studies, because of their special character, remain outside these categories.

Holders of a degree of technical secondary school and final secondary school (science section) would be admitted to these schools, as would also, under certain conditions, those graduating from a professional school with degrees of technical ability and holders of the traditional secondary school degree (Maturita).

Those who have the "Scuole Superiore" degree will be permitted to enter the university to acquire the degree of "Laurea" in those branches corresponding to the type of study chosen in the first level of higher education.

Special care should be taken to facilitate the passage between the Faculty and the "Scuole Superiore" and vice versa. In this way the following results would be obtained: (a) those who are not very apt to pursue university studies will be guided towards practical studies; thus there will be a sort of orientation and selection right from the first years of study; (b) this will check the phenomenon of repeated failure; and (c) greater access to the universities by admitting, through "scuole superiore," candidates who otherwise do not possess any special diploma or degree usually required for admission to the university.

Consequent to the introduction of the "scuole superiore" and the ability of its graduates to enter the university, it will be necessary to reorganize the studies

Table 3-20

Italy: Evolution of the Number of Students for the Period 1965-1970
(public schools)

Academic year	Elementary school	Lower Secondary school	Classical Sec.Sch.	Technical school	Professional schools	Art Schools	Universities
1962-63	4,042	1,451	277	345	140	13	226
Period 1965-70							
1965-66	4,190	1,760	350	470	190	16	280
1966-67	4,230	1,850	360	490	210	17	310
1967-68	4,260	1,940	355	500	240	18	330
1968-69	4,310	1,990	350	510	270	19	345
1969-70	4,380	2,030	350	530	300	20	360

of the Laurea. In particular, the Minister cites the example of the schools for engineers which, at a national level, have created a five-year course composed of two years, followed by a three-year course for which the curriculum will be composed of specialized subjects, some of them compulsory and others which can be chosen by the student.

The detailed organization of studies, for the moment, would be left to the faculties.

5. The introduction of the pure research doctorate, without professional goals, recognizes the urgency and importance of research, and brings with it a profound transformation of the university structure. The introduction of "dipartimenti" (departments) is being considered, because at the level of scientific research the department can comprise within its body scientists coming from various disciplines and faculties, permitting better cooperation and offering a better organization for the preparation of the research doctorate.

However, the introduction of departments and the research doctorate should not diminish the importance of postgraduate studies which have as object higher professional specialization.

6. It is undoubtedly possible to proceed to an elaboration and precision of the university's autonomy, but it seems much more important to improve its functioning; therefore one would enlarge the role of the representatives of businesses and of the citizenry naturally interested in the good functioning of the university, in the Managing Committee and increase the authority of this committee. Representatives of the board of professors and assistants would also be represented in this committee. As for the students, they would be represented with a consultative voice in the councils concerned with the "social mission" of the university.

7. The plan warns that it will be difficult to both increase the professor/student ratio and increase the professional qualifications of the teaching staff during the rapid expansion of higher education unless increased financial means are dedicated to teacher training. The plan provides, over a period of six years, for the creation of 9,600 teaching posts, with an annual increase of 1,600 professors, assistants, etc.

8. The plan provides also for the creation of new university institutes in various regions of the country; for example, in the region "Piemonte" (Torino – highly industrial) will be created a "Scuole Superiore" (first level of higher education) for engineers.

Conclusion. The whole of noncompulsory education is conceived in the "Linee direttive" as a professional training on a short-, medium- and long-term basis. This conception corresponds to the necessities of an industrialized society. Some observers believe that the general spirit of the plan will destroy the prejudices concerning the superiority of a classical education and will spread the idea that only aptitude should decide whether the professional training of an individual is to be on a short-, medium- or long-term basis: this should diminish the errors in orientation caused by the traditional prejudices.[43]

However, Italian noncompulsory education remains divided into three sections, as in the past, and entrance into the university for those not holding the traditional degree for entrance remains problematic, since the "Linee direttive" do not specify the conditions under which graduates of the technical and professional institutions will be permitted to attend the university.

But an important new element is brought forward by the Minister's plan:

The relationship between culture and professional qualification is perceived in the "Plan Gui" in new terms. Culture is no longer an autonomous fact independent of professional qualification. Professional qualification is conceived as a cultural expression of which the general training constitutes the essential element while the specialization represents an additional specification. This presents the "Linee direttive" from being maintained "in too timid and backward a position in comparison with the degree of evolution of the problem, and it introduces into the perspective of the development of the Italian school a new dynamic force: the principle that any professional training is above all the result of a sufficiently broad general training.[44]

It appears to us, however, in the light of the principles, quite similar to those of the "Linee direttive," laid down by the Langevin-Wallon commission in 1946, that principles are one thing, and their implementation another. Specifically, we are thinking of the great vacuums in the "Plan Gui" with regard to the criteria which will define the orientation of the students to the various levels of higher education, and the criteria which will enable, for example, a graduate of the "Scuole Superiore" to attend the university. However, our reservations with regard to the "plan" are less strong because of the unquestionable value of the "scuola media" which should diminish considerably the inequalities of "chances" offered to the children and improve the orientation process.

With regard to the economic factor, in 1959 the SVIMEZ (Associazone per lo sviluppo dell'industria nel Mezzogiorno — Association for the Industrial Development of the South) concluded a study relating to the likely changes in manpower requirements during the next fifteen years which compares the percentages of the different levels of skill and training of the active population in 1975 to the percentages of the distribution of an age group among the different levels of education. This method, as pointed out by Raymond Poignant,[45] has the disadvantage of taking as its basis the structures of 1975, which are only a moment in a continuous evolution. As the "Linee direttive" do not specifically refer to this SVIMEZ study, it is difficult to conclude that they were based partly on this study; nevertheless, because of the examination of the Investigating Commission's suggestions by the National Council for Economy and Labour, one could reasonably believe that the manpower requirements were taken into consideration extensively, although they are not explicitly mentioned.

Furthermore, one should note Italy's participation in the OECD's "Mediterranean Regional Project," which was set up by bilateral agreements between OECD and the governments of Greece, Italy, Portugal, Spain, Turkey, and Yugoslavia, and "which represents an attempt by national research teams to assess the implications of economic and social objectives on the size and distribution of requirements for education in the period up to 1975.[46]

In his forward to the Italian national report for the "Mediterranean Regional Project," Gino Martinoli, president of the Study Commission for the school program, indicates that in Italy efforts towards the formulation of a policy of development of the school structure have preceded the efforts dedicated to economic planning which have only been undertaken from 1963-1964 onwards, whereas, as we have seen, the basis of a national development plan for education was laid down in 1959 with the "ten-year plan." However, here again it is not clear whether the "Linee direttive" were themselves inspired by the OECD report.

4

Education, Students, and Change

Coming to the end of this study of higher education in Europe, two dimensions stand out: "professionalization" (more accentuated in France and Italy, and highly influential in their planning) and "organized democratization," dimensions which find their origin in the social and economic development of Europe.

We shall now analyze how this evolution and the introduction of these new dimensions affect and mark the European student, especially in his choice of studies and the modes of teaching that we mentioned in a previous chapter.

Today the students receive a university education whose ends no longer correspond to their aspirations:

The present university structures are those of a liberal and humanist university whose goal is not to form 'cadres' but rather to mold cultured gentlemen . . . traditional values have been contradicted by economic realities which have deprived them of any real meaning. The university is no longer creater but depository; university education is no longer a collective participation in the creation of a living culture but a transmission from generation to generation of a dead culture.

This analysis quite accurately represents, with the necessary nuances, the opinion of the European student leaders (Belgian, French, and Italian in particular). Presented in a more concrete and more constructive manner, this critique implies:

the necessity for the acquisition of knowledge corresponding to the present development of science and technology . . . to these requirements for theoretical training are added requirements for technical training; an initiation into the methods and techniques of the profession must be included in higher education. An initial polyvalence is indispensable in order to permit the inevitable reconversions and adaptations which will mark the course of professional life . . . A training based on professional development is thus not limited to the acquisition of professional techniques; it contains from the beginning a scientific training of fundamental importance. For us, the theoretical training must take precedence over the need for technical training. In order to permit the acquisition of a critical spirit and of a methodological sense, we must also learn how to learn.[1]

So the educational program cannot be limited to the training received at the university; it must allow the various cadres of the economy, teachers and researchers especially, to acquire the critical abilities with respect to their scientific discipline and to the techniques of their future occupation (which implies, among other things, education in the evolution and classification of the sciences and in the history of technology), and also with respect to the socio-economic structures in which they will work (which in turn necessitates economic and sociological study). Consequently, the "necessity for a general education, for a polyvalence of all cadres lends us to reject the splintering of higher education into several separated structures."[2]

A Unified University with
Diversified Internal Structure

The justified apprehension provoked by the diversification of higher studies, as it is presently conceived of in certain countries, is not, as we have seen, limited to the students. In the course of our study we have seen representatives of the academic world and of public authority express a desire to give every student a basic training which would permit his fullest development. Nevertheless, we have noted in France, with the creation of the Institut Universitaire de Technologie, and in Italy, although to a lesser degree, with the "Scuola Superiore," a tendency towards specialization and quickened professional training. In France, moreover, the IUT's as they are presently conceived, have not obtained the approval of academic authorities who are doubtful about the possibility of training a middle-level cadre in so short a period of studies. But underneath this doubt we sense the feeling that the training given is too technical in its inspiration and organization.

This diversification of higher studies brings to mind the similar fate of secondary education in the course of the 19th century.

Formerly, the criteria which were supposed to classify the student were badly or not at all defined. Too often it was social and economic position which determined the type of secondary study, often to the detriment of students coming from middle and lower social classes (petite bourgeoisie, tradesmen, workers) whose parents were not accustomed to orienting their children in the direction of higher studies. Will it not be the same within a specialized higher education? And, with even graver consequences? For, not only will the short cycles, in which studies are based mostly on professional development, attract children from modest-income families, because of the professional and intel-lectual aspirations characteristic of these families, but even worse, the training received will not permit the individual to adapt himself to the new requirements of his profession and of the society, due to the lack of theoretical knowledge, not to mention the lack of cultural education permitting the full development of the person. But the question remains open and only the results of the short cycles will teach us about the quality of the education dispensed in these institutions cut off from research and about the types of students recruited.

For the moment, it seems that the debate between liberal university and technocratic university has been left behind to the extent that the first has been rejected, if not for ideological reasons, then at least because it does not correspond to the evolution of the needs of modern society, and that the second is denounced as harmful to the full development of the individual, who will in the course of his career be the victim of the short-view professionalization.

The adaptation of the university to the economy is, for many, an irreversible process and not a short-term policy whose scandals and deficiencies it would suffice to denounce. "The political expression of this process has been given us by Minister Fouchet (French Minister of Education) from whom we borrow these two key formulas: 'to place the student in the service of the university' and 'to industrialize the university.' "[3]

In Europe today, in the face of this short-term professionalization of higher education and the very tentative democratization of the university, the student, or at least his leaders, have become more conscious of being dependent on socio-economic factors. The opening of higher education to students from more modest social classes has brought about a change of attitude toward study. For a son of the upper bourgeoisie, the university represented an intermediate phase between strict family obedience and the adult stage of succession to the father or entry into the controlling spheres of the nation. The studies themselves as a result were much less important than "the life of a student." Recently a study notes that the choice of "exotic" themes and areas of study becomes more frequent the higher the student's social origin.[4]

On the other hand, the student from less favored social classes will be more attached to his university work and be characterized by a greater dependence on the university. Because his future is not assured (it depends on academic success in the first place and on professional success subsequently), he cannot allow himself "the elegance of detachment and the risks of virtuosity."[5]

However, along with the growing economic independence of the student from his family (the number of 'independent students' is growing: 30 percent on scholarship, 40-50 percent doing night or part-time work) comes more independence on the cultural plane and in the choice of a profession.

The father's occupation can thenceforth no longer dominate the future nor even be valid as example, whether it belongs to a backward economic sector, or no longer gives sufficient income, or involves very specialized labor. The sons of the doctor, lawyer, and engineer will no longer necessarily be doctors, lawyers, and engineers, or, at least, if they are, it will not be because their fathers were, but because of the very necessities of economic evolution and the growing specialization required in all the disciplines.[6]

The student has, of course, a class origin which directly influences his social and academic attitudes, but he cannot have a class-determined life project nor identify himself with his class of origin, (for its social, economic, and cultural determinants are no longer his own. "What characterizes the situation of the student is his present conditioning, in which his familial and social past are a factor as well as the future that he glimpses, the vision that he has of himself once his studies are completed," remarks Mark Kravets, then Secretary-General of UNEF and now of the Mutuelle Nationale de Etudiants de France.

Thus, at the moment when ties with his family are relaxed, the future remains uncertain. The student floats between two worlds. He has a specific autonomous consciousness of his condition, reaffirming the opposition of the heir to his family traditions, uncertain of his outlets but conscious of his rights. Opposition, but not divorce, because the son of the family desires his liberty. The future is less certain, the competition sharper, the working conditions difficult for all. Privileges, to a great extent, have fallen. And the educational phase of life has become a "social state or condition." Becoming conscious of this state gives rise to a new solidarity.

Is there a student class? The phrase is too strong for an occasional and diverse group. Their pasts are not common and their destinies diverge. It would be a curious class which is emptied and reborn every four or five years. It would be more appropriate to speak of an "age class," for the dimension youth plays as much role in the group feeling of the students as the dimension intellectual. This student class exists more subjectively, by the phenomenon of identification with the milieu and in the consciousness that the student has of belonging to a homogeneous group.

But an ambiguity remains. The student does not lose all feeling for his roots and can have in him, as a result, a "conflict of milieus": the family and the university. Student "syndicalism" thus seeks a statute (not in the sense of a piece of legislation but rather a socially accepted status), which would define the place and the autonomy of the student within society. The UNEF has found this formula: "young intellectual worker." Here is manifested the desire for solidarity with the working class and, it might be said, the "intellectual's complex": to have a bourgeois heart and a socialist head. For the student of the left the difficulty is so much the greater, as the future promises make him a high-level cadre; in the marxist conception, a servant of the bourgeoisie.

The politically moderate student escapes this conflict, for he sees in his studies only a phase and not a state. University work is for him the beginning of a bourgeois career. He rejects any alliance with the workers and asks of the public powers only that they facilitate his professional life. He is "a future cadre of the nation" (the definition adopted by the Federation nationale de Etudiants de France). The two formulas — that of UNEF and that of FNEF — are opposed term by term: "young" and "future" (desire or refusal to identify with the present), "worker" and "cadre" (notions which imply different mythologies and systems of alliance), "intellectual" (part of the traditional vocabulary of the left) and "nation" (part of the traditional vocabulary of the right).

The new independence of which we spoke, accompanied by a feeling of increased responsibility and, perhaps, of growing insecurity, leads the student to take a more active part in the organization of a system of which he is the product.

The fact that student groups in Europe demand from institutions and public authorities better material conditions of work (instructors, classrooms, libraries, lodgings, financial assistance) has lead many to think that these were the essential demands of the students, who would thus be acting in a corporatist spirit. Thus, George Gusdorf, Professor at the University of Strasborg, said, "It is absurd to imagine that all will be for the best in this best of all worlds because the unit price of a meal in the university restaurant will have fallen by 21.05 centimes, because the popular soup of a free and obligatory polycopied course will have been distributed to all comers, or because the last loiterer of the two year program course will have been assured of a stool."[7]

It seems to us that student demands go far beyond these material preoccupations and bear equally on the right of determining educational programs, even contesting the omnipotence of the examination. Paul Fraisse, Professor of Experimental Psychology at the Sorbonne, remarks:

The key to this system of education, which permits, in the majority of cases, the judgment only of qualities independent of the material itself, e.g., techniques of memorization and exposition . . . (there is an) uneasiness which has, for a number of years, troubled the relations between students and professors . . . the general atmosphere of the relations between professors and students alters from year to year . . . the students no longer lay the blame solely on the university administration or public authorities. They directly question the instructors, their methods and their attitudes.

It is interesting to note two examples of this evolution in student demands. We take first the events at the University of Berlin because they took place in a country where the idea of the democratization of education is quite recent and finds application only with difficulty in the social and political context of liberal Germany, which is now discovering what Le Monde calls, "the student-citizen."

Student agitation at the Free University of Berlin — reputed to be progressive — caught the attention of political observers in the course of a series of incidents which opposed the students to the Rector (who is the spokesman of the Faculty Senate which, in fact, directs the university and in the work of which two students participate. The U. of Berlin is, moreover, the only one where this very limited "coadministration" exists). The conflict was over meetings of a political character organized by the students. The sanctions taken against a faculty member further increased the tension. The faculty member had claimed in a Berlin daily newspaper that the philosopher Karl Jaspers was prevented from speaking at the university because of his unorthodox opinions on the German question. In 1966, the Le Monde correspondent reports, there was a confusing controversy over the rules: can and/or should the University Senate refuse the use of communal places to meetings and demonstrations of a political nature?

But the student demands go far beyond the framework of the "right to free speech." At the same time that their journal *FU-Spiegel* systematically criticizes authoritative courses and pedagogical insufficiencies of some distinguished professor, it also states:

The students demand to be more closely associated with the actual administration of the university; we will facilitate, under the form of the teach-in, discussions which bear on tabooed subjects or dismantle some official mystifications; finally, we proclaim that the community of teachers and of students so much vaunted is not a flock of sheep bleating under the shepherd's staff . . . (At Berlin, also, one is warned against a university) fabricater of diplomas, in charge of disgorging specialized functionaries at lowest price.

In the Netherlands, Belgium, and Italy we find in student milieus the same uneasiness and the same demands, although they are not always expressed in the form of a battle program of student unions, as is the case in France and Italy.

The Union Nationale des Etudiants de France (UNEF) analyses the present situation, in its "Manifesto for a democratic reform of higher education," with respect to university structure, the content of education, pedagogical methods, and the status of the student. This student organization especially denounces teaching methods:

It is still the didactic method which dominates the organization of education; the course excathedra which permits no dialog between student and teacher is still the foundation of teaching... This absence of dialog reduces study to an apprenticeship in established knowledge... excluding most of the time any possibility of criticism. The dogmatism of the magistral course implies an absence of teaching in methodology. The professor, sole master of education, requires above all a good knowledge of his course.

The students denounce the existence of a situation in which they can only be passive, "cram" the course, compose the few essays asked from them in the course of the year, and then, on the day of the exam, present, as best they can, what the professor was able to expose from the height of the podium. They have had enough of this — at least at the level of the leadership — and demand methods of work: "give us techniques . . .!"

Paul Fraisse, Professor of experimental psychology at the University of Paris, summarizes the situation in these terms:

Our students have grasped more rapidly than their mentors the change undergone by the university as its scale changes. The latter is no longer asked to form the intellectual elite of an aristocratic or bourgeois society; it is charged rather with preparing the cadres of a country in full demogrphic and technical expansion. The majority of the young men that it accepts are of voting age, sometimes married, burdened with a family, living more or less well. They find themselves ill at ease in the atmosphere of the faculties where they have the impression, rightly or wrongly, of being reduced to the state of docile and passive schoolboys. In the "university-factory" they feel alienated: the education dispensed to them has been conceived for them but without them. Whence comes their recent attacks against the most venerable of university institutions, the magistral course. The time is past when the disciple formed himself after the example of a prestigious master. Lost in a vast auditorium, hardly hearing the professor's voice, the student prefers polycopies, demands a dialog with an assistant closer to him, and presses for small study and learning groups.

This coming to consciousness is an important fact and contains the germs of a pedagogic revolution. For the professors themselves are seeking a reform of university work, which, on the one hand, would give a role to the magistral course and would, on the other hand, coordinate the latter with practical work done within groups of smaller size.

The student seems to be seeking methods of work elaborated in the spirit of a large, but precise, cooperation, if not with the professor, because that seems to be impossible in present material and financial conditions, then at least with the assistant-master, and especially with his colleagues through practical work and, in particular, within working groups directed by the students themselves. In France, for example, these are called Groupes de Travail Universitaire (G.T.U.):

In these groups the students compare their products and methods of working; the G.T.U. prepare the students for group work, which constitutes an important aspect of professional activity, and give them the possibility of acquiring a certain autonomy in their work . . . The university should facilitate their creation and functioning by putting at their disposal the necessary small halls and by organizing sessions of initiation into methods of group work in the course of classes, in particular, at the beginning of the year.[8]

The presentation of these demands, suggestions, and reactions, which are certainly of considerable importance, calls forth a number of observations.

In the first place, this very intransigent expression of the desire for direct participation in university work — from the elaboration of programs to pedagogic methods to examinations — may only be the feelings of a minority. On this point we would like to cite at length the experience of J. W. Lapierre, presently in charge of the sociology conference at the University of Madagascar, but at Aix-en-Provence at the time of the incident:

I am not ignorant of the fact that student syndicalism demands some quite spectacular changes in teaching methods. But my experience has shown me that there is unfortunately a considerable gap, and some contradictions, between the requirements expressed by student organizations and the effective behavior of the majority of students; which is, of course, not surprising: the militants of student syndicalism form an active minority which does not always succeed in carrying the majority along behind it. Three years ago, at the Institute of Political Studies of Aix, I made a loyal attempt to follow the method extolled by student syndicalism. I had, for one optional course, thirty students. I replaced the magistral course by a polycopied course which was put into the hands of the students. At each weekly session I designated a certain portion (30-40 pages) of this course to be read and studied for the following week, asking that questions, critical observations, or extensions be presented by the students in order to create a methodical discussion. Now, I was too quickly to verify that more than half of the students did not do this preparatory work and thus could not participate in the discussion. Some of them, whom I directly provoked in order to draw them out of their passivity, showed by their response that they had not even read the thirty pages of polycopy. By the second semester the group was reduced to twenty: a core of regular and active participants (a half-dozen), several regular but passive listeners (another half-dozen), and a public as passive as fluctuating, made up of those who came from time to time, which was almost never the same from one time to the next. The examinations were on the whole rather bad. In the preceding years, the magistral course on the same material had been followed more regularly and the results of the final examinations showed on the whole a better assimilation of knowledge.[9]

It is obviously difficult to draw any conclusions from a single testimony, although some other attempts of the same type have been made with apparently the same results. On the other hand, it is clear that the teaching staff, although it always expresses the most lively satisfaction in seeing the students more active in his course of studies, retains no less the impression that the student is by nature passive. This is a very wide-spread idea, even outside of the university, and Raymond Poignant reaffirms it in terms that could not be clearer:

The students ... do not know what they want, with the exception, perhaps, of being assured good employment upon leaving the university. During meetings of the Commissions on the Plan, in which representatives of the students participate, we asked them to speak about their problems, ... but they could not even articulate them.

Is it really only the student who is to blame? Here is one comment: It is a known fact that the European student, following a more than 150-year-old tradition which confers upon him liberty in the organization of his studies, a tradition which, by the way, is more comfortable installed in myth than in daily practice, feels repugnance for all pedagogic methods which would reinforce the subjugation that he denounces elsewhere and would be contrary to his idea of the noble labor of the intellectual novice. Moreover of all the professorial functions, the most regularly forgotten – as much by certain professors as by certain students – is without doubt the continuous organization of the exercise as an activity directed toward the acquisition, as completely and as rapidly as possible, of the material and intellectual techniques of intellectual work. Tacit accomplices, professors and students agree often to define at least cost the tasks properly expected of them. To recognize the liberty of the student and to pretend to see in him, throughout the year, a free, or better, autonomous, worker, i.e., capable of imposing on himself a discipline, of organizing his work, and of holding himself to a consistent and methodical effort; this is the price that the professor must pay in order to see returned by the student thus defined the image that he tries to give and have of himself as master of thought and not as pedagogue or pedant, as teacher of quality for students of quality. To require continuous presence at the course or the punctual filling of responsibilities would be to annihilate the professor and the student at the same time, such as they see themselves and wish to be seen by the other.[10]

Thus this "ideal of cooperation" is only rarely encouraged in the tradition of the European university. Collective work can only exceptionally find support from university institutions. Among the tasks that they assign themselves, the professors often relegate to the lowest rank the function of organization which is incumbent on them, more particularly, the task of framing the collective work of the students; moreover, the schools inculcate from infancy a contrary ideal, that of individualistic competition. So, should the students express to the university the wish to do work in teams formed by them, they are in no way prepared to invent techniques which would contradict values interiorized so long before. The frequent failure of university working groups results from the fact that the students cannot, even by a miracle of resolution, create, exnihilo, some new forms of integration.[11]

Several observers, among them Bourdieu and Passeron, are in agreement that the student, deprived of institutional frameworks, is also deprived of social frameworks, and is more and more distant from student traditions, from "the student folklore which has integrated, at least symbolically, the student milieu." We observed this transformation in France and Italy, but to a much lesser degree in Germany, the Netherlands, and Belgium, where the traditions remain lively. But is not out of the question that the next few years will witness an evolution in these countries approaching that manifested in France.

Everywhere that university life has developed, it has marked a geographic district which retains a great originality. Thus, there are student quarters, student cafes, and student rooms .... But one has only to walk in the famous Latin Quarter of Paris to verify that this place cannot furnish by itself a framework of integration. Certainly, the example of Paris is not definitive, because the conditions of life of the student are exceptionally difficult there, as a result of the very existence of "monster Paris" (a third of all French students live there).

Nevertheless, a place which should be more favorable to the integration of the student milieu — a university city — scarcely offers a more favorable image of this hoped for result. We have particularly long and interesting experience in this matter, having been directly confronted with these questions as president of the students of the Cite Universitaire of Paris — and it was an unfortunate experience. The administrators, as well as the student Leaders, had to acknowledge the inertia that they met whenever they addressed themselves to the students. We remember in particular the remarks of an illustrious foreign visitor and great friend of the Cite, a professor in a Mexican university, who exclaimed at a meeting of the Administrative Council, "But the Cité is becoming a dormitory . . . ."

We have been in a position to verify that if contacts are established between students it is not thanks to a geographic milieu or to the fact of sitting together at some courses, but that they rest much more on some exterior social ties, especially geographic origin, preceding scholarly experience (at the level of secondary school), political or religious convictions, and according to Bourdieu and Passeron, common belonging to higher social classes.

All of the sociometric tests show that exchanges outside of the classroom and even the simple knowledge of names are extremely rare. If, as different indices suggest, the most consistent and diverse exchanges are the act of students coming from the upper class, it is, as a thousand other facts testify, because they are more at ease in the university milieu and also, perhaps, because they derive from their previous education some techniques of sociability which conform to such a milieu. A limited poll taken at Lille seems to indicate that, all other things being equal, it is the students, both male and female, from the highest social levels who are the best known by their comrades and, although to a lesser degree, know the greatest number of them in turn. Equally, the act of seating oneself near to the podium being taken as a sign of ease and confidence, it is not surprising that, whatever type of acquaintance is envisaged (from knowledge on sight up to cooperation), the number of co-students known decreases regularly as one goes from the first rows toward the back of the hall.[12]

In summary, "the student milieu is perhaps less integrated today than ever . . ." To this statement we would like to add: yes, this is true, but only if we take into consideration the institutional and social frameworks which are characteristic of the European university and its students. At the precise moment when the student acquires greater independence and realizes to what extent he is tributary to a social and economic context with new needs, he begins to seek new means of integration. It seems to us that the demands that we have revealed, as well as those which refer to a "student salary" and student accommodations, express the refusal to accept this "disintegration" and the will to search for new factors which might favor integration.

Monetary Allocation for Studies

With the new independence of the student, some new perspectives are opened, of which the demand for a monetary allocation for studies is one of the expressions. (This demand was first adopted at the Congress of Arcachon of the UNEF in 1950; a legislative proposal based on it was deposited by the political party SFIO (socialist) at the National Assembly in 1956 and the Federation of the Democratic Left, led by Francois Mitterand, took it into its program of July 14, 1966.)

It starts from the idea that when the student enters into higher education he aspires to greater liberty and greater personal responsibility — aspirations which have for too long been muzzled by the organization of secondary education in Europe. But the liberty that he finds there, which consists mostly of "laissez-faire" and limited professorial concern, is this true liberty? The answer seems to be no. For the student at the university remains an object to be taught.

Magistral courses, practical work, and exams, compound their effects and outline the narrow contours of a permanent cycle: take notes, learn, recite .'. . excluding any initiative. Not only is he not welcome in the process of organization of studies and determination of programs, but even the exercises which are the frame for his daily work make him a professionally passive and irresponsible individual; to know the magistral course as well as possible — a necessary condition for success at the end of the year — to do a yearly report in the framework of the practical work . . . so many thankless tasks, pure repetition of different trials for the exam, buried in a formalism which favors the swelling of the program and the necessity of doing all of it.[13]

Consequently, personal labor is inevitably parallel to university work; the second becomes an extra task, an imposition, all the more so as the material to which it is applied does not appear to be logically chosen as a function of any rigorous finality; the content of teaching, most often unadapted to the professions to which it gives entry, accentuates the irresponsibility of the student by hiding from him the raison d'être and purpose of his work.

The state of material dependence presently created by the financial situation of the typical student is felt more directly than the irresponsibility of his studies. The desire to have a personal budget and to manage it autonomously appears before university age; but, once this age is reached the need is rendered even more lively by a certain latitude in the organization of existence, while the financial dependence remains — dependence on the family and on the state.

Aid from family remains the basic element in the student budget, more or less important according to social category of origin (as shows a most serious study undertaken in France by the Mutuelle Nationale des Étudiants de France, MNEF, and published in "Recherches Universitaire," No. 6, 1964). This fact would seem to have some grave consequences, e.g., one might suppose that the uneasiness felt by the student in depending on his family while at the age of normally providing for one's own needs could cause him to pursue a course of study which is neither too long nor too difficult, running the risk of not responding to his own best interest and desires. Also, the student might choose certain studies because they are dispensed nearer to his family home, reducing costs of lodging and/or transportation.

State aid does not resolve the problem, for there again the student obtains a scholarship as a result of social criteria, of the material situation of *his* family; he does not owe it to his own work but to the precariousness of the material situation of his family. "We do not want chairty" is a phrase heard often in random trips through the student communities of Europe, a phrase which summarizes well the feeling of dependence. Finally, loans and pre-contracts serve only to tie the student more closely to certain private enterprises and public organizations. The loan is a commitment heavy with consequence, since it makes the pressure for academic and professional success so intense that the student feels this responsibility as a heavy burden. The present system of assistance corresponds to the conception of the student held by society, which does not wish to recognize that his activity has real social utility.

"Night work," performed by 33 percent of French students, and vacation work, helping 25 percent, are condemnable in themselves, since in the majority of cases they correspond neither to his studies nor to the profession to which the student is destined. Furthermore, it has a bad effect on success in study and personal initiative, especially when it occupies a great part of the student's time and provides an essential share of his resources.[14]

This schematic presentation of the material situation of the student allows us to consider the question of his status — (status having the implication of legal or customary acceptance) — a status which can presently be defined as the absence of a status. There is, in effect, a specificity of the adolescent condition, of the condition of a young man who is physiologically adult but not professionally and socially, who is held in a state of dependence by the fact that he does not yet have the intellectual and economic means which would permit his integration in a positive and active manner into the society. As Andre Gorz remarks:

From the fact that it presently takes between five and eight years to form a highly qualified professional worker, it follows then an individual who would have been adult at the age of fifteen or sixteen in an archaic society is still, in a highly developed society, an adolescent, a minor. The student experiences this contradiction between his physical maturity and his social subjugation as a form of oppression. It is inevitable that it be this way.[15]

It can already be seen that the allocation for study is not only for the satisfaction of essential material needs, nor that the demand for it can be considered as "the corporatist reflex of a relatively privileged group." This demand tends to open larger perspectives for the student and is founded on the new social function and role of the university.

This larger perspective is expressed by the rapprochement between the intellectual worker and the manual worker, who have convergent claims, whether it be a question of occupational formation, of the opening of the university to all the workers, or of the human formation that integration into every civil community requires.

If the students demand a salary for study, it is because they judge that the student conditions impart the economic and social expansion of the collectivity and that "one can, therefore, speak of the differential productivity of student labor." In addition to the attempt to bring together all the young workers, manual, and intellectual, there is also the search for types of social relations comparable to those which will mold the life of the ex-student, as soon as he has fully entered the labor force.

In this direction, student leaders consider lodging as an essential element in the formation of the "young intellectual worker." They denounce the university cities and the campuses (which have made their appearance in Europe, re-grouping the restaurants and living quarters around the places of work), because they cut the student off from the external world and because this architectural conception rests upon a schematic vision of the life of the student, who is thought to be "entirely occupied by work or by sleep." So, they demand types of lodging which permit more contact with other social groups. To this effect, it is necessary to mention the action taken by the MNEF with respect to its experimental lodgings. As two investigations of Le Monde (September 1947) and June 1948) revealed, the 120,000 students of France, of whom 5 percent are tubercular, "are the passive victims of the inflation" of the postwar period. Scholarships are derisory in number: only 6,000 in 1947 and the sums received remain largely insufficient. The directors of UNEF set themselves two objectives, the salary and social security. The second was soon obtained by the law of September 22, 1948, which extended social security to students; the law is part of the policy of social progress elaborated during the years of the resistance and it bestowed upon the students themselves the responsibility of managing their system of social security. The creation of the Mutuelle Nationale des Etudiants de France dates from this time. This measure should not be considered only from the point of view of ameliorating the material and health condition of the students, for it seems also to have expressed the desire to situate the problems posed by the condition of the student in a totally new perspective. It is only to the extent that the students are considered to form a homogeneous group, defined by a common situation and common needs, that the institution of a particular regime of social security for them makes sense.

The MNEF has essentially two sorts of activity: on the one hand, the management of the regime of student social security and, on the other, the implementation of a health policy more adapted to the student milieu. In the matter of prevention diverse initiatives have been taken: the creation of bureaus of psychological aid (BAPU), made necessary by the importance of mental hygiene in the student environment; the operation, in three university cities, of centers of gynecological consultation and family planning; participation in the administration of the "Foundation Sante des Etudiants de France," created to run a sanatorium for tubercular students built by UNEF in 1923, where all the material facilities needed to pursue their studies are available during the period of convalescence. Today the foundation possesses fifteen establishments with four more in construction.

The annual budget of the MNEF is more than two million dollars, in addition to the social security funds which it administers, and financing is assured by an assessment (20F per student) and by a commission from social security. It employs full time more than 300 persons (non-student).

In France, where the problem of student lodging in particular and the problem of housing in general is often posed in a dramatic fashion, the programs adopted by the Mutuelle are characterized by the constant effort to implant student housing within the city. Thus, there are three successive experiences to be noted in the action undertaken by the Mutuelle, which disposes of 866 movable housing units, the majority of which it owns:

1. The purchase of apartments within a new complex of buildings, most of the time converted into collective housing; in particular, reserved for young couples. This attempt has not yet given satisfying results, especially because of the difficulty that so many of the students experience in establishing permanent contacts, in the absence of socio-cultural facilities.

2. Creation of student cities, where too often cultural liveliness is absent because of the absence of facilities, but where the Mutuelle continues to try.

3. The construction of a building run by the Mutuelle in an area of the city with cultural facilities. Here, it is necessary to mention the "Tour de Grenobles" (a university town in France) with thirteen stories destined to hold thirty student families and ninety-six single men and women. To the Tower are joined a cafeteria, a lecture hall, and a library, also constructed by the MNEF, which should make the student residence an attraction for all the inhabitants of the neighborhood. This complex, which has the attention of architects and social psychologists as well as educators, in which responsible students are called upon to participate actively in associations and administrative councils of groups based in the area, should provide the experience which would permit the development of a policy facilitating the integration of the student into his own residence and into the non-student milieu around him. The Mutuelle offers to the residents the management of their own city, their cultural activities, and the use of their time; all these being aspects of the life of an individual and of a collectivity which are refused to the residents as a group in the cities of the Centre National des Oeuvres (state owned and operated).

The segregation of student housing from the surrounding habitations is the policy which guides the majority of projects of university implantation today. In opposition, the Mutuelle has developed a form of student lodging integrated in a non-university ensemble in which the student is offered great possibilities for participation in the collective life of the neighborhood.

Thus, we could say that there are, and always have been, two tendencies in the programs of student organizations. One is concerned with the defense of the particular interests of the students, i.e., "corporatist" or "businesslike." The other is concerned with attempting to open larger perspectives to the student by the establishment of contacts with the world of labor and the greater world outside, and beyond this contact, action leading to the satisfaction of the convergent needs of the young workers, intellectual and manual, i.e., to a "revendicative syndicalism." In truth, however, the distinctions to be established are more complex and have to do more with the "objective conditions" of mass action in the student situation and the relations of the leadership to the base.

The UNEF was, if not in crisis, at least the theater of serious quarrels which have not to this day been settled. The majority within its General Assembly[a] demands that the UNEF launch a far-reaching campaign to obtain the allocation for study, while the minority wants a battle against the university reforms now in operation. Is there an incompatibility of objectives here? The two factions do not think so; the former declaring that it is also in favor of a structural reform and the latter that nobody could suspect it of being hostile to the student salary. It is surely, then, a quarrel which conceals differences over syndical strategy, fundamental differences, as an observer has remarked, "one guesses the presence of that old sea serpent: reform or revolution?"[16] But "the students are bewildered. The famous strategic debate is followed by no more than 300 or 400 of them. One hundred thousand held membership cards in UNEF last year; this number has probably fallen to 80,000."[17]

In order to present an example of these "objective conditions," of, if one prefers, of the divergence between the "conditions of work" and "conditions of life," we present below the response of two students who are members of syndicates and militants of UNEF to an article by Marc Kravets, in the review Les Temps Modernes, titled "Naissance d'un Syndicalisme Etudiant," on the subject of university working groups (G.T.U.). (These groups are proposed by UNEF and are meant to allow students to work together on specific problems so as to exit from excessive individualism and moral solitude):

When Kravets speaks of the work groups as offering either 'a possibility of situating themselves politically in the process of transformation of society' or the opportunity 'for participating instead of submitting,' one has the impression that he oscillates between the marxist model of the proletariat and the romantic image of creative work and living culture. For lack of having defined the limits of group work, of having shown that it should not be taken so much as a "reversal" as one means among all those of which the student disposes, and a means always subordinated to the professor, Kravets makes it appear more as an ideological proposition than as a practical method. This is inscribed in the very movement of his text, in which the work group is introduced not for itself, but "in parallel" with battles, as 'a positive expression of the taking in charge by the students of their own problems.' To define culture at the student level and the work group as creator is from the start to place oneself beyond the student problem. This excessive position makes him see only 'passivity' in the present condition of university education.[18]

---

[a]The General Assembly is composed of representatives from the Associations Generales d'etudiants — A.G.E. There is one of these associations for each university center, with the exception of Paris where there is one for each higher-educational establishment. The members of the A.G.E. are elected and in turn elect some of their own members to serve in the General Assembly of UNEF.

Kravets, who represents the "minority" within the UNEF, saw the question in a global perspective:

If you put to the side the global purpose of action — a new model of education, of culture, of insertion of the intellectual worker into the society, thus a new type of society — what do you oppose to the Fouchet plan? Some more rational technical solutions which, in order to be realized, would prohibit any perspective on the totality; or some day to day demands with regard to rooms, housing, scholarships, and assistants?"

The relative politicizing of students in Europe and the vivacity of their search for the absolute, for a debate at any price, in a word, the student condition would merit consideration at greater length, but this would be to overflow the boundaries imposed upon us in this chapter, namely, to study the consequences of university reforms and socio-economic evolution as they manifest themselves presently in student milieux.

Nevertheless, we must mention in conclusion that the present tendencies seem to be inspired by the demand for an education open to all the citizens providing a general culture and a better professional qualification. The preoccupations of the students, despite the diversity of currents which animate them, are in the spirit of the Langevin-Wallon Commission, which also praised a larger opening of the university and its members to the mass of workers, in light of the following idea: "General culture represents that which brings men closer together and unites them, while profession represents too often that which separates them."

General Conclusions

Our purpose has been to present and criticize the way in which the countries of the European Economic Community have dealt with the challenge of the modernization of the educational system and its adaptation to the economic, social, political, and human needs of our times.

In so doing we have presented and clarified the European university tradition, the actual structural situation of the university, the reforms proposed and occasionally applied, the problems and discussions that these reforms have provoked, and finally the evolution of student society and its effects on educators and education.

At the present stage of development and internal differentiation of the university, any general overview that one might offer would be probably erroneous. Nevertheless, certain particular elements can be retained.

The first such element, which is for some the basic source of *the* challenge which faces the university today: "how to become a mass institution and at the same time keep the initiative of innovation and quality in every domain . . . ." is the increase in the total number of students. The quantitative revolution in European higher education — as well as education at other levels — is the result of a spontaneous upsurge in demand for prolonged education and the expression of a new image of social success. Is there any reason why this general movement should be expected to stop? The expansion is part of a general economic expansion and development of technology, bringing new requirements for professional qualification, and perhaps is also parallel to a search for higher cultural standards by the European population.

Moreover, the forecasting of economic and social needs over the next twenty years gives no reason to reduce the output of highly qualified professionals. To the contrary. Even at present levels of development the Common Market countries are losing the race for graduates. They produce, in absolute figures, about one-quarter the number of the United States and one-third the number of the Soviet Union. Part of this difference can be ascribed to differences in population, birthrate, and per capita income. But the evaluation of the number of graduates per age group of equal size continues to reveal important disparities: 4 percent of an age group in the Common Market as against 5.6 percent in Great Britain, 8.2 percent in the Soviet Union, and 19.6 percent in the United States.

Furthermore, the very creation and development of the Common Market (the theory of the "extent of the market"), leading to the development of industries too large for the confines of a single small country and to increased specialization and division of labor, will stimulate the need for qualified personnel and impose new demands on education. The time when National Manpower Commissions of the Planning Commissions will have to make their evaluations in terms of the needs of the Common Market as a whole is not very far off. A first attempt to pose the problem in these terms — although not explicitly — is the report of the Institute for University Studies of the Common Market, "Education in the Common Market Countries," directed by Raymond Poignant, which was undertaken at the request of the Action Committee for a United States of Europe. (This latter Committee is presided over by Jean Monnet and contains representatives from most of the political parties and trade unions of the E.E.C. countries.) Consequently there seems, from the economic point of view, to be no reason for the expansion of all types of education to case or not be encouraged.

Apart from these needs for qualified personnel, there remains what is probably the fundamental role of the university: to contribute to the democratic ideal while upholding "high culture" through its teaching and research, a "high culture" the access to which still remains the privilege of a few.

We have seen the reforms applied during the past few years at the level of secondary education whose purpose it is to open this type of education to more children of the lower classes while strengthening the means of selection and orientation. These procedures are deemed insufficient by numerous educators who demand a "common core or trunk" in order to reduce the cultural inequalities between children of diverse social origins, and are judged too strong by others prejudiced in favor of the "aristocratic culture."

In France presently and shortly in Italy, and their example is likely to be followed in time by the other countries, a system of diversified higher education is being instituted which itself necessitates a method of selection and orientation; the latter operating either within the last year of secondary education or during the first year of higher education.

Without rejecting in itself the idea of diversified university education, one can with reason ask whether the reforms involving what could be called multiplication of channels correspond to the intellectual and technical exigencies of our time. When an "Institut Universitaire de Technologie," or a "bacalaureaat," or even a "Scuola Superiore" is created, is it not implicitly admitted that these new establishments are far from the university and are to be run on principles foreign to it? Is this truly university education? Is it not simply the possibility of pursuing a longer course of studies, which is in the end only an exigency imposed by the new techniques and which has some precedents in the history of education in Europe?

Thus, we are led to reconsider the mission of higher education and the democratic ideal. For this purpose we cite at length an authoritative source,

In the present state of society and of pedagogical traditions, the transmission of techniques and habits of thought required by the school falls in the first place on the family milieu. Any real democratization presupposes that they be taught where the least favored are able to acquire them, i.e., at the school, and that one enlarge the domain of what can be rationally and technically learned through a methodical apprenticeship at the expense of that which is abandoned irredeemably to the chance of individual talent, i.e., in fact, to the logic of social privilege . . . The pedagogic interest of students coming from the least favored classes . . . resides in requiring from the masters that they "shoot the breeze" instead of presenting an exemplary and inimitable prowess suitable for making the students forget that this grace is only a laborious acquisition or a social heritage. . . .

. . . The rational pedagogy is yet to be invented and should in no way be confounded with the pedagogies presently known which, having only psychological foundations, serve a system which is ignorant of and wishes to ignore social differences. Nothing is thus further from our minds than to appeal to the so-called scientific pedagogy which, increasing in appearance the (formal) rationality of education, permits real inequalities to press more heavily than ever, with more justifications than ever. A truly rational pedagogy would have to be founded on an analysis of the relative costs of different forms of education (courses, practical work, seminars, work in groups) and of the diverse types of pedagogic action of the professor (from simply technical assistance to effective direction of student work); it would have to take into account the content of education or the professional ends of training and, envisaging the diverse types of pedagogic relations, it must not forget their differential productivity according to the social origin of the students. On any hypothesis, it is subordinated to the knowledge of socially conditioned cultural inequality and to the decision to reduce it.[19]

On the other hand, in this version of the mission of higher education there is a tendency to make no distinction between the "spirit of research," which consists essentially in a systematic curiosity of the spirit, and "the activity of scientific research," which is the thorough exploitation of the former.

It seems to us then that the problem of higher education, its development, its pedagogic conceptions, and its diversification is situated at these two levels: a rational pedagogy and the formation of young men in such a way that from the first years of education this "spirit of research" is stimulated. A spirit which, according to André Boulloche, former Minister of National Education in France, is impregnating all of modern life: "We must form young men who systematically question life, and this formation must come very early in the educational process."

Diversification, as it is presently conceived of in Europe, and democratization without this "rational pedagogy" can correspond only to a democratic ideal which limits itself to satisfying only a single aspect of human needs: to give man a professional qualification permitting the amelioration of a precarious material situation, but leaving untouched his vast cultural needs and the methods of research and reflection that he has always intuitively wanted but that a combination of economic and social conditions bring today within his grasp for the first time.

And yet, it is certain that these tasks require considerable human and material means that no government is presently in a position to furnish. At least that is what Michel Bosquet (Andre Gorz) thinks:

... In Europe per capita wealth is a third or half of American wealth and it is impossible to extract funds at the same time for the integral development of education, the construction of armaments, and especially the type of opulent consumption which, following the American model, is being diffused; thus for Europe there is, from all the evidence, a contradiction between the priority given to the so-called economy of opulent consumption and the needs for social investments. This is true not only for education but for all collective equipment, whether it is a question of hospital equipment or of regional development or even of full employment; there is an incompatibility between the mass diffusion of motor vehicles, of durable goods of the washing machine type, and, on the other hand, consumption of national education. If a head of government or party chief in Europe claims to give priority to national education, that means that he must, if he is logical with himself, impose a redistribution of resources at the national scale; he must attack the mechanisms of capitalist accumulation.

In summary, the University in Europe remains to be made; not a technocratic university, as some fear, nor a liberal university, but a democratic and humanist university, a humanism for the industrial world. It is without doubt because that implies choices of capital importance for our world that the debates are so passionate, the discussions so sharp, and that important decisions are retarded and substituted by reforms wherein hides the eternal devil of adaptation.

Bibliography

Bibliography

Aron, R., "A propos de la crise de l'Universite," *Le Figaro,* April 2, and 6, 1964.

Bourdieu P. and J. C. Passeron, *Le Heritiers, les etudiants et la culture,* Paris, 1964.

Bowles, F., "Rapports preliminaires recueillis par l'etude internationale d'admission a l'Universite," in *Aspects economiques de l'Enseignement Superieur* (Groupe d'etude sur les aspects economiques de l'enseignement), OCDE, Paris, 1964.

Cavazzo, F. L., "The European School System," *Daedalus,* Winter, 1964.

Creutz, E., "La democratisation des etudes est-elle un leurre?" Centre d'information et d'education populaire du mouvement ouvrier chretien, Bruxelles, 1965.

Decaunes, L. and M. L. Cavalier, *Reformes et projets de reformes de l'enseignement francais de la Revolution a nos jours* (1789-1960) Paris, 1962.

Delcroix, F., "Les etudiants dans le tunnel," *Le Nouvel Observateur,* No. 9, Paris, January 14, 1965.

Deniau, J. F., *Le Marche Commun,* Paris, 1961.

D'Hoogh, C., *Evolution structurelle et democratisation des etudes a l'Universite Libre de Bruxelles,* Bruxelles: Institut de Sociologie de l'Universite Libre de Bruxelles, 1965.

Duverger, M., "La reforme des etudes de droit," *Le Monde,* November 26 and 27, 1961. "L'Avenir des Facultes: un numerus clausus," *Le Monde,* May 20, 1964.

Edding, F., "Planification de l'Enseignement Superieur en Republique Federale d'Allemagne," in *Aspects economiques de l'enseignement superieur* (Groupe d'etudes sur les aspects economiques de l'enseignement), OCDE, Paris, 1964.

Friis, H., "Introduction," in *Organisational Problems in Planning educational development* (Study Group in the Economics of Education), OCDE, Paris, 1966.

Fourastie, J., "Les donnees economiques du probleme de la planification," in *Planification et Enseignement,* Paris, 1963.

Girard, A., H. Bastide, and G. Pourcher, "Enquete nationale sur l'entree en sixieme et la democratisation de l'enseignement," *Population,* Jan.-March, 1963.

Girard, A., "Les donnees demographiques du probleme de la planification," in *Planification et Enseignement,* Paris, 1963.

Harmel, P., L'element humain dans l'economie, experiences communes a diverses regions du monde. Semaines sociales de Versailles, Lyon, 1958.

Koch-Kijlstra, M. J., "Vernieuwing van het wetenschappelijk onderwijs in Hederland," *Universiteit en Hogeschool,* No. 6, Utrecht, July, 1963.

Kravetz, M., "Naissance d'un syndicalisme etudiant," *Les Temps Modernes,* No. 213, Paris, February, 1964.

Jaccard, P., Politique de l'emploi et de l'education.

Langevin-Wallon (Le Plan) de Reforme de l'Enseignement, Compte rendu du Colloque organise par le groupe francais de l'Education nouvelle et la Societe francaise de Pedagogie, Paris, 1964.

Mast, A., *Les pays du Benelux,* Paris, 1960.

Parnes, S. H., *Forecasting educational needs for economic and social development* (The Mediterranean regional project), OECD, Paris 1962.

Piekaar, A. J. and J. Nittel, "L'Enseignement superieur aux Pays-Bas," in *L'Enseignement Superieur en Europe, France, Pays-Bas, Pologne* (Etudes et documents d'education, No. 49), UNESCO, Paris, 1964.

Piobetta, J. B., *Les Institutions universitaires,* Paris, 1961.

Poignant, R., *L'Enseignement dans les pays du Marche Commun,* Paris, 1965. "France, the Planning of Education in relation to economic growth," in *Policy Conference on Economic growth and investment in education,* Washington, 16th-20th October, 1961, OECD, second printing, Paris, 1966. "Establishing educational targets in France," in *Planning education for economic and social development* (the Mediterranean regional project), OECD, Paris. "Les problemes poses par la planification dans l'enseignement," in *Planification et Enseignement,* Paris, 1963.

Postma, E. B. J., "Baccalaureaatsopleiding voor leidinggevende functies in het bedrijfsleven," in *Universiteit en Hogeschool,* No. 4, Utrecht, March, 1964.

Reguzzoni, M., *La reforme de l'enseignement dans la Communaute economique europeenne,* Paris, 1966.

Svennilson, I., F. Edding and L. Elvin, "Targets for education in Europe in 1970," in *Policy conference on Economic growth and investment in education,* Washington, 16th-20th October, 1961, OECD, second printing, Paris, 1966.

Thomas, J. and J. Majault, *L'Enseignement primaire et secondaire. Tendances actuelles et problemes communs,* Conseil de la Cooperation Culturelle du Conseil de l'Europe, Strasbourg, 1963.

Thomas, J., "Les tendances de la planification de l'enseignement en Europe," in *Planification et Enseignement,* Paris, 1963.

Vermot-Gauchy, M., *L'education nationale dans la France de demain,* Monaco, 1965.

Woltjer, H. J., "Studieduur en studieregeling," in *Universiteit en Hogeschool,* No. 6, Utrecht, July, 1959. "De Universiteitsgedachte als actueel probleem," in *Universiteit en Hogeschool,* No. 4, Utrecht, March, 1961. "Verkorte studieduur als algemeen universitair en meatschappelijk probleem," in *Universiteit en Hogeschool,* No. 5, Utrecht, May, 1958. "Idee, Gestalt un Aufgabe der Universitaten in den Niederlanden," in *Universitat und Moderne Welt, Ein International symposium,* Berlin, 1962.

Collective Works, Documents, and Publications

Annales parlemantaires de Belgique. Senat. Compte rendu analytique, seance du jeudi 25 juin 1964.

Avenirs, Revue mensuelle, No. 133 (June, 1962) and No. 154 (July, 1964) Paris.

Budget (Le) de l'etudiant. Recherches Universitaires, No. 6, Paris, 1964.

Cashiers de l'Union nationale des etudiants de France, No. 7 & 8, Paris, 1966.

Committee on Higher Education: Report of the Committee appointed by the Prime Minister under the chairmanship of Lord Robbins 1961-1963, London, HMSO, reprinted, 1965.

Condition(La) socio-economique de l'etudiant de l'enseignement technique superieur en 1963-1964, Centre d'Etudes des problemes sociaux et professionels de la technique, Bruxelles, 1965.

Dossiers documentaires, Institut Pedagogique National, No. 77, November, 1965, Paris.

L'Education nationale. Revue hebdomadiare d'information pedagogique, Paris, 10 fevrier 1966.

Educational Planning. International Bureau of Education, XXVth International Conference on Public Education, Geneva, 1962.

Enseignement(l') aux Pays-Bas, in the collection Notes et Etudes Documentaires, No. 3021, la Documentation francaise, Paris 23 septembre 1963.

Enseignement(l') en Belgique, in the collection Notes et Etudes Documentaires, No. 3169, la Documentation francaise, Paris, 8 mars, 1965.

Enseignement(l') en Republique Federale d'Allemagne, in the collection Notes et Etudes Documentaires, No. 2973, la Documentation francaise, Paris, 16 mars 1963.

Enseignement(l') en Italie, in the collection Notes et Etudes Documentaires, No. 3100, la Documentation francaise, Paris, 27 juin, 1964.

Faire l'Universite. Dossier pour la reforme de l'enseignement superieur. Espirit, Houvelle serie. Paris, mai-juin 1964.

Finanziamento del piano di sviluppo della scuola nel quinquennio dal 1966 al 1970. Senato della Repubblica – IV Legsilatura. Disegno di legge (N. 1543). Communicato alla presidenza il 21 gennaio 1966.

Foundation Universitaire, Bureau de Statistiques Universitaires, Rapport Annuel, 1965, Bruxelles.

Forecasting manpower needs for the age of science, EOEC, Paris, 1960.

Guide des systemes scolaires, Conseil de la Cooperation culturelle du conseil de l'Europe. Strasbourg, 1965.

Il costo-tasse nelle Universita statali. Ricercha e documentazione No. 1, Consorzio Universitario nazionale Italiano cooperative Librarie editoriali, Roma.

Linee direttive del piano di sviluppo pluriennale della scuola per il periodo successivo al 30 giugno 1965, by Minister Gui by the terms of the law of July 24, 1962, No. 1073, Ministero della Pubblica Instruzione, Roma, September 30, 1964.

Moniteur Belge, Bruxelles, April 27, 1965.

Mouvement(Le) educatif pendant l'annee scolaire 1964-1965, Rapport succint du Ministere de l'Education Nationale et de la Culture, XXVIIIe Conference internationale de l'instruction publique, juillet 1965 Brussels.

Nota naar aanleiding van de ontwikkelingsplannen van de Universiteiten en Hogescholen voor het tijdvak 1963-1966, Brief van de Minister van Onderwijs en Wetenschappen (Zitting 1964-65, 8131), The Hague.

Planification(La) de l'enseignement en France, in the collection Notes et Etudes Docuemnatires, No. 2935, la documentation francaise, Paris, le 9 novembre 1962.

Principes de la planification del 'enseignement, Etudes et Docuemnts d'education, No. 45, UNESCO, Paris, 1963.

Project(Le) regional mediterraneen: Six pays en quete d'un plan; Espagne, Grece, Italie, Turquie, Yougoslavie; OCDE, Paris, 1965.

Publications de la Mutuelle Nationale des Etudiants de France, Paris (rapport annuels, notes d'informations).

Quatrieme Plan de developpement economique et social (1962-1965), Rapport general de la Commission d'equipement scolaire, universitaire et sportif (Commissariat General du Plan d'equipement et de la productivite, Paris 1961).

Rapport sur la croissance des populations estudiantines, Conseil National de la Politique scientifique, Brussels, 1961.

Rapport annuel, 1965. Conseil national de la Politique Scientifique, Bruxelles, 1965.

Rapport sur l'expansion et l'adaptation de l'enseignement superieur de niveau universitaire, Conseil National de la Politique Scientifique, Bruxelles, 1964.

Reforms and innovations in Dutch University Education, Ministry of Education and Science, The Hague, 1965 (Docinform 162).

Spens (The) Report, H.M.S.O., London, 1938.

Relazione della commissione di indagine sullo stato e sullo sviluppo della pubblica instruzione in Italia, vol. I: Testo della relazione, Ministero della P.I. Roma, July 24, 1963.

Relazione sullo stato della pubblica instruzione in Italia, presented by Minister Gui by the terms of the law of July 24, 1962, No. 1073, Ministero della P.I. Roma, March 31, 1964.

Spreiding van het Universitair Onderwijs in Vlaanderen, Ruimere Kansen voor allen, Antwerp 1964.

Uitleg, Weekblad van het Departement van Onderwijs en Wetenschappen No. 1, September 21, 1965, The Hague.

De Spreiding van het Hoger Onderwijs tot 1970, Rapport. Universiteit en Hogeschool, No. 4, Utrecht, February 1960.

Nouveau(Le) regine de l'acces aux etudes universitaares (Loi du 8 juin 1964), Ministere de l'Education Nationale et de la Culture, Bruxelles.

Vie(La) scientifique dans la Republique Federale d'Allmagne, Essen-Bredeney, (Stifterverb and fur die Deutsche Wissenschaft).

Wissenschaft in Daten, Jahrbuch, 1962, Stifterverband fur die Deutsche Wissenschaft, Essen-Bredeney.

Notes

Notes

Chapter 1
The Problematic

1. Fabio Luca Cavazza, "The European School System," *Daedalus* (Winter, 1964), p. 395.

2. Michel Vermot-Gauchy, "L'education nationale dans la France de demain," *Monaco* (1965), p. 14.

3. Ibid.

4. Raymond Poignant, "Les problemes poses par la planification dans l'enseignement," in *Planification et Enseignement*. Paris: IPN, p. 14.

5. As quoted from: Fabio Luca Cavazza, "The European School System," *Daedalus* (Winter, 1964).

6. Reforms and innovations in Dutch University education, Ministry of Education and Sciences, Docinform 162 (The Hague, 1965), p. 21.

7. Conseil National de la Politique Scientifique, Brussels, Rapport sur l'expansion et l'adaptation de l'Enseignement superieur de niveau universitaire (March 23, 1964), p. 71.

8. Robbins' Report, London, 1964.

9. Institut de sociologie de l'Universite de Bruxelles, Evolution structurelle et democratization des etudes a l'Universite libre de Bruxelles (Brussels, 1965), p. 30.

10. Ibid.

11. Bulletin, International Association of Universities, November, 1964.

12. Robbins' Report, Appendix Five, p. 89.

13. Robbins' Report, Appendix Five, p. 113.

14. Arts and Loisirs, no. 24 (Paris, March 9-15), p. 3.

15. Nederlandse Studentenraad, Leyden, Memorandum adopted with the "smallest possible majority" on April 19, 1965.

16. UNEF, P. J. Coquerelle, 1965.

17. J. Fourastie, "Les donnees economiques du probleme de la planification," in *Planification et Enseignement,* IPN, Paris – cycle de conference, brochure no. 19 MS, p. 44.

18. Ibid. (page preceding) p. 44.

Chapter 2
Democratization

1. Raymond Poignant, "Les problemes poses par la planification dans l'enseignement," in *Planification et Enseignement,* Paris: IPN, p. 275.

2. As quoted from Fabio Luca Cavazza, The European School System," *Daedalus* (Winter, 1964), p. 401.

3. The Spens Report, London, 1938.

4. Fabio Luca Cavazza, "The European School System," p. 400,

5. Michel Vermot-Gauchy, "L'education nationale dans la France de demain," *Monaco,* (1965), p. 271.

6. Ibid., p. 273-274.

7. Michel Vermot-Gauchy, "L'education nationale dans la France de demain," p. 67.

8. Ibid., p. 65.

9. Raymond Poignant, "Les problemes poses par la planification dans l'enseignement," pp. 283-284.

10. Fabio Luca Cavazza, "The European School System," p. 396.

11. P. Harmel, "L'element humain dans l'economie; experiences communes a deverses regions du monde." Semaines sociales de Versailles. Editions de la Chronique Sociale de France (Lyon, 1958), pp. 13-14.

12. Ibid.

13. Manifeste pour une reforme democratique de l'enseignement superieur, Union nationale des Etudeants de France (UNEF) (Paris, 1965), p. 14.

14. H. J. Woltjer, "Idee, Gestalt und Aufgabe der Universitaten in den Niederlanden," in *Universitat und Moderne Welt, Ein Internationales Symposion* (Berlin: Walter de Gruyter & Co., 1962).

15. Ibid.

16. Friedrich Edding, "Planification de l'Enseignement Superieur en Republique Federale d'Allemagne," in *Aspects Economiques de l'Enseignement Superieur,* OCDE, Groupe d'Etudes sur les Aspects Economiques de l'Enseignement.

17. H. J. Woltjer, "Idee, Gestalt und Aufgabe der Universitaten in den Niederlanden," p. 356.

18. Edding, "Planification de L'Enseignement Superieur en Republique Federale D'Allemagne" pp. 171-172.

19. Ibid.

Chapter 3
Planning and Finances

1. In OECD, Establishing Educational Targets in France. Planning Education for Economic and Social Development, pp. 205-206.

2. Raymond Poignant, "Les problemes poses par la planification dans l'enseignement," in *Planification et Enseignement,* Paris: IPN, p. 208.

3. Philip H. Coombs, "Educational Planning in the Light of Economic Requirements," in *Forecasting Manpower Needs for the Age of Science* (Paris: OEEC, 1960), p. 26.

4. Poignant, "Les problemes poses par la planification dans l'enseignement," p. 210.

5. International Bureau of Education, Geneva and UNESCO, Paris: "Educational Planning," XXVth International Conference on Public Education, Publication No. 242 (Geneva, 1962).

6. Ibid., p. 114.

7. Ontwikkelingsplan R. U. Leiden, Introduction, p. 2-3, as cited in "Nota Naar Aanleiding Van de Ontwikkelingsplannen Van de Universiteiten en Hogcscholen."

8. International Bureau of Education, p. 58.
9. F. Edding, Aspects Economiques de l'Enseignement Superieur, (Paris: OCDE, March, 1964), p. 159.
10. "Empfehlungen des Wissenschaftsrates zum Ausbau der Wissentschaftlichen Einrichtungen," Teil I, Wissenschatlichen Hochschulen.
11. Edding, Aspects Economiques de l'Enseignement Superieur, p. 167.
12. Ibid., p. 172.
13. M. Reguzzoni, La Reforme de l'Enseignement dans la Communaute Economique Europeene (Paris, May, 1965), p. 83.
14. International Bureau of Education, p. 54.
15. Raymond Poignant, "France," in *The Planning of Education in Relation to Economic Growth,* Policy Conference on Economic Growth and Investment in Education, (Washington, 1961), Paris: OCDE, January, 1966, p. 10.
16. Poignant, "France" (The section on Mission, Composition and working methods of the Committee are based on this report).
17. J. Fourastie, "Les Donnes Economiques du probleme de la planification," in *Planification et Enseignement,* Cycle de Conference (Paris: IPN, 1963), p. 44.
18. *Le Monde,* July 28, 1965.
19. Poignant, "France," p. 23.
20. Ibid., p. 25.
21. Ibid.
22. Ibid.
23. Raymond Poignant, "Establishing educational targets in France," in *Planning education for economic and social development,* Paris: OECD, p. 220.
24. Ibid., p. 208.
25. XXVth International Conference on Public Education, Geneva, 1962 – Educational planning, Research in Comparative Education, Belgium, pp. 12-13.
26. Ibid.
27. Annales Parlementaires de Belgique. Senat Compte rendu analytique, seance du jeudi 25 juin 1964, p. 627.
28. Annales Parlem. de Belgique. Senat. Compte rendu analytique, du 25 juin 1964, p. 627.
29. International Bureau of Education, p. 85.
30. Ibid.
31. Ibid.
32. Mario Reguzzoni, "La reforme de l'Enseignement dans la Communaute Economique Europeenne (Paris, 1966), p. 209.
33. Ibid., pp. 238-239.
34. A. Natta, "Ancora al di qua della reforma," in *Riforms della scuola* (Jan., 1964), p. 5, and as quoted in M. Reguzzoni, Ibid., p. 239.
35. Relazione sullo stato della pubblica istruzione in Italia, Ministerio della Pubblica Istrusione (Rome, March 31, 1964).

36. Ibid, p. 12.
37. Ibid., p. 14.
38. Ibid., p. 66.
39. Ibid., p. 68.
40. Ibid., p. 84.
41. Linee dirrettive del piano, op. cit, p. 15 ff.
42. Ibid.
43. Reguzzoni, "La reforme de l'Enseignement dans la Communaute Economique Europeenne," p. 256.
44. Ibid., pp. 257-258.
45. Poignant, "France," p. 23.
46. Gino Martinoli, The Mediterranean Regional Project, Reports by Country (Italy: OECD, June, 1965), p. 5.

Chapter 4
Education, Students, and Change

1. In UNEF Programme (supplement to 21/27 "The French Student.")
2. Ibid.
3. Marc Kravets, "Naissance d'un Syndicalisme Etudiant," in *Les Temps Modernes,* No. 213 (Feb., 1964).
4. P. Bourdieu and J. C. Passeron, *Les Heritiers-les etudiants et la Culture* (Paris: Les Editions de Minuit), pp. 29 and 31.
5. Ibid., p. 41.
6. See Note 3 above.
7. G. Gusdorf, *L'Universite en Question* (Paris, 1964), p. 76.
8. Program UNEF.
9. In *Esprit,* May-June, 1964.
10. See Note 4 above.
11. Ibid.
12. Ibid.
13. See Note 8 above.
14. MENF in *Rechereches Universitaire,* No. 6, 1964.
15. In *Journal de la Cite,* No. 4, January, 1966.
16. Francois Delacrois, "Les Etudiants dans le tunnel," in *Le Nouvel Observateur,* No. 9 (January 14, 1965), p. 2.
17. Ibid.
18. M. Briand and J. P. Briand, "Sur les Problems etudiants," in *Les Temps Modernes,* No. 216, May, 1964.
19. Bourdieu and Passeron, *Les Heritiers-les studiants et la Culture,* pp. 119-120.

About the Authors

About the Authors

Eric Bockstael is a Belgian-born journalist who studied economics, law and letters in Paris. He has traveled widely in the United States and has taught at Monteith College and Wayne State University.

In his student days he was president of the Cité Universitaire in Paris.

Otto Feinstein, associate professor of the Science of Society Division, Monteith College, Wayne State University in Detroit, was born in Vienna, Austria, in 1930. He graduated from the University of Chicago, spent three years at the Graduate Institute for International Studies in Geneva Switzerland, and returned to the University of Chicago for his Ph.D.

He is the author of *Two Worlds of Change,* Anchor Press, 1964 and *Michigan Economic Myths: Defense Contract, Employment and Affluence;* Wayne-Monteith Monographs, 1962. He is editor of *New University Thought* and has written articles for numerous publications. From 1963 to 1966 he was the Director of the Danforth Study: *Higher Education Economics — Quality and Personalism,* from which the current work is drawn.

Professor Feinstein is interested in the workings of nonmarket institutions and the theory and practice of resource allocation to explicit and implicit value goals of these institutions. This thread of concern runs through his works in the economics of higher education, defense economics, and United States-Latin American relations. He is currently working on a study dealing with the impact of Vatican II on the Roman Catholic Church in Ireland.